God WANTS YOU CLOSER TO Him

God Wants You Closer to Him

ROBIN L. CONNERS

Pleasant Word
A Division of WINEPRESS PUBLISHING

Pleasant Word (a division of WinePress Publishing, PO Box 428, Enumclaw, WA 98022) functions only as book publisher. As such, the ultimate design, content, editorial accuracy, and views expressed or implied in this work are those of the author.

Unless otherwise noted, all Scriptures are taken from the *King James Version* of the Bible.

Hard Cover:
ISBN 13: 978-1-4141-1147-6
ISBN 10: 1-4141-1147-9

Soft Cover:
ISBN 13: 978-1-4141-1345-6
ISBN 10: 1-4141-1345-5

Library of Congress Catalog Card Number: 2007909566

With God stretching out his arms to you, with the outpouring of his tremendous love for you, his child, above everything, wanting you closer to him, I dedicate this book to you, the reader. You are to be commended and complimented for making the personal choice to hunger and thirst to be closer to God.

God's Spirit lives within you and is shared with others by your love for God and all of his children, who are all of your brothers and sisters in Christ Jesus.

May the words of this book touch your heart, mind, and soul, and make you a loving inspiration to your fellow man of God's love, all through the name and shed blood of his Son, Jesus. Amen.

ACKNOWLEDGMENTS

A VERY SPECIAL THANKS to God our Father, Jesus, the Son of man, and the Holy Ghost, who has been my inspiration, comforter, loving companion, and mentor, giving me the thoughts and words to share with you, so you may personally feel and know the love of God for you, along with the power and presence of God himself.

Also, I'd like to say a very special thanks to my loving wife, Rose, who has stood beside me for many years in faith and in love for me as a person, and who has prayed for me on a daily basis. Thanks also goes to our son, Ryan: as he has grown through the years, he has taught me to be a better person through being the best father and provider that I can be, setting the example for him.

Finally, I'd like to say a special thanks to all my Christian brothers and sisters in Colorado Springs, Colorado, for all their love and support throughout the years. There is such a prevalence in their inner being of an extension of the love of God's spirit.

CONTENTS

PREFACE

THESE WRITINGS ARE given to you, the reader, to strengthen and encourage your walk into God's Kingdom. You will be asked to pray out loud and experience closeness with God by doing what is asked of you in different paragraphs. It's important that you do these actions and say these prayers with love and understanding. Different terminologies or meanings will be given to help you understand how to do and say these actions and prayers. By practicing the different actions and by praying for what you need, you will benefit as you read this book. Many times we do not understand how to do things, and we just need to be told how to do them.

I pray you will receive these words into your heart and mind, as they are written with God's love within me and my best intentions. These writings are intended to give you, the reader, a personal experience with God. You may need to read certain parts over and over, and ask God to help you to understand and to open your mind to receive this understanding, always asking in the powerful and inspirational name of Jesus.

Please pray the following prayer:

> Dear Heavenly Father, in the name and shed blood of your Son, Jesus, please open my mind, heart, and spirit to receive everything that you would like for me to receive in the reading of this book. Amen.

INTRODUCTION

THROUGH THE WRITINGS in this book, readers will learn the ways God wants people to get closer to him. This transformation takes place in your heart, mind, and spirit through knowledge, belief, faith, and prayer. God does in fact want you closer to him. The way to get closer to him is by understanding his words in the Bible and how to apply them in your everyday life. This book will use the life experiences of the author as puzzle pieces, showing how to put them together to see what the picture looks like. This picture shows how God is speaking to him; therefore, it can show each and every person—especially you, dear reader—how God is personally speaking to you.

Reading this book will give you a unique experience: the experience of a loving God speaking to you on a one-to-one basis. Simply pray for God to give you understanding each and every time you read it. This will prepare your heart and mind to be in an understanding state and to be filled with God's love. Satisfaction will come by reading and understanding his true word to you at each reading.

A person is required to come to God's table and eat of his word continually to truly experience his love. God's ultimate goal for your life is a personal, one-on-one relationship of love and guidance.

Many people are hungry and thirsty to see God at work and to really figure out a way to get to know him. God has spiritual principles that govern the way the world operates. All you have to do is ask him for understanding through his Son, Jesus, believe you have received, and God will open your mind to see and come unto an understanding of him. God's principles are spread throughout the Bible. You will discover in this book a condensed synopsis of his principles through examples and how they apply and are at work all around you without your even knowing it. You, too, will see for yourself that God is truly working in your life to get your attention. Understanding comes a little bit at a time as a person's heart is being changed, molded, and transformed.

The readings in this book will give you new life and energy as you will be changed forever. This change will come by the hand of God himself. When you realize this change is taking place within your heart, mind, and spirit, praise and thank God for his presence, love, and mercy upon you, dear reader.

Note: All Scripture quotations come from the King James Version of the Bible.

Chapter One

YOU AND GOD

GOD WANTS YOU closer to him so you will understand and realize that he loves you so very much. God loves you a lot; he truly loves you. Repeat this three times out loud: "God loves me." Very good, now say it again, just a little louder this time: "God loves me." Now, one more time, dear reader: "God loves me." Doesn't it feel good to know God loves you? It does feel good, it feels really good. Now thank God for being there for you all of the time. "Thank you, God, for being such a loving God." In your personal faith in God, he wants you to know that he truly loves you and always will. With this love he wants you to be closer to him by obeying his commandments. There are ten of them. They can be found in the book of Exodus, chapter 20, beginning with the third verse.

Talk to God

God wants you to talk to him in prayer. Thank God, honor God, and praise him. Just start out by saying:

> Thank you, God, for everything I have. Thank you for my friends, my family, my possessions, my health, the fresh air that I breathe, the beautiful day ahead, and all the things that I have.

There are people out there, you know, who have less than you do. Here is another example:

> Thank you, Lord God, for this beautiful day, for the song birds to listen to, for wonderful people, for the crisp and clean air that we breathe, for the beautiful sky, and for the rains to feed our crops and plant life. Thank you for my loving family, and thank you, God, for being my best Friend and spiritual Leader.
>
> Father God, I honor you and praise you; you are my everything. In the name of your Son, Jesus, please bless the people that have hurt me. God, please bless ______ (say the names of the people that have hurt you in your prayer), as these people were hurtful to me. I ask that you bring them closer to you, and I forgive them for what they have done to me. I know that the battle is not of flesh and blood, as it states in the Bible, "For we wrestle not against flesh and blood, but against principalities, against powers, against the rulers of the darkness of this world, against spiritual wickedness in high places."
>
> (Eph. 6:12)

Speak Life to Others and Yourself

God wants you to speak life unto others and yourself, for the tongue has the power of life and death. It states in the Bible, in Proverbs 18:21, "Death and life are in the power of the tongue: And they that love it shall eat the fruit thereof."

What do I mean by this? Well, when you are talking to someone, or a group of people, you do not say profane or insulting words. For instance, you do not call a person "an idiot," because you are telling that person he or she is not very smart, when in the person's own way, he or she is very smart, because that is the way God made him or her.

Start training yourself to speak well of people. Do not talk about what people do to you or to others. This wastes your time, and it keeps you from doing the good God wants you to do. Do not talk about bad things happening to other people, because God wants you to draw closer to him by encouraging others and building others up instead of trying to destroy others. The second commandment is to love one another. The book of John says, "This is my commandment that ye love one another, as I have loved you" (John 15:12), and it says, "These things I command you, that ye love one another" (John 15:17).

Sowing and Reaping

Speak well of one another, and treat one another well. Whatever you plant by your words or deeds, you will ultimately harvest yourself. If you speak well of one another, then you will be spoken well of. You reap what you sow, as it states in the Bible, "Be not deceived; God is not mocked: for whatsoever a man soweth, that shall he also reap" (Gal. 6:7).

This is probably the most important scripture in the whole Bible. Think about this: If I steal from someone, then, according to this scripture, I can expect to be stolen from. By stealing from someone, I am supporting the influences of theft; therefore, I am promoting these same influences around me. This means that I can expect to be stolen from. In the same way, if I lie to others, then I should expect to be lied to.

This scripture applies to both good and bad words and deeds. Sometimes people have to see the bad that may happen to them if they keep doing bad things. This is something to be feared. Remember—you reap what you sow; you get what you give; what goes around comes around; what you plant is what you will harvest. If you plant a weed with your voice, you are going to get a weed. You will not get a beautiful flower. If you plant a seed with your voice by saying someone is going to get fired, then you can expect to get fired. If it is okay for someone else to be fired from his job, it is also okay for your boss to find a reason to fire you, because the words you spoke revealed your heart.

Be careful what you ask for, as it may very well come true. If I, as a parent, keep calling my child's mistakes dumb, my child will probably start thinking he or she is dumb. On the other hand, if you start talking about only the good things that a person does, you will discover all the good things that happen when you say and do good things for others. My challenge to you is this: speak only of the good things that people say and do. Remember that when you give life with your mouth, you will receive life. Pray for blessings from God for other people, and you will receive blessings from God.

Many times we have to pray against a certain behavior that is not pleasing to God and then pray for a blessing to surface. Once you have prayed a prayer for someone, believe by faith that it has happened, and keep believing. For example, you can pray for someone with an alcohol problem by saying something like this: "Dear God, in the name of your Son, Jesus, I ask that you remove the desire to drink alcohol from (name of person), and I pray that you will bless his (or her) life as he (or she) becomes closer to you. Bless him (or her) with your love."

Have Empathy for Others

God wants you to get closer to him by having empathy in your heart for your fellow man. What is empathy? It is a much-desired part of you that God wants you to strengthen. You practice empathy by placing yourself into a person's situation. Pretend that you are the one in his or her situation, and notice how this makes you feel.

For example, say someone makes a promise, and then he or she finds an excuse not to keep that promise. The person who made the promise should place his or herself into the shoes of the person who was promised, so that he or she knows the impact of the broken promise on that person. Say, for instance, that I tell someone I will give him or her $5.00 for gasoline if he or she takes me to the grocery store 15 miles away. Then, after we get back from the grocery store, I say, "I do not have it now and will have to give it to you in 2 weeks, because I spent more than I should have on food." Then in two weeks I say, "Oh, I do not have it. I will have to give it to you next week," and next week never comes. Well, the person who received the promise of money probably feels like, "Why would someone say something and then not do what he or she said he or she would do?" Put yourself in that person's shoes—how does the broken promise make that person feel? Is the money so important that a person should lie and not give the $5.00?

It is important to do what you say you are going to do. Sometimes, others may misunderstand what you say you are going to do. Get it clear in the beginning—clarify what is going to be done, how it's going to be done, and when it will be finished. God wants us to love one another.

Empathy is directly related to giving and receiving with understanding the other person's perspective of a certain event or situation. This is related to God's principle of sowing and reaping. One day you may want someone to understand the position you are in and give you a helping hand. So you should try to understand others' points of view.

Empathy is a great form of loving your brother or sister. An entire chapter can be written on empathy and the effect it has on people around us. Imagination is great for the mind, and many times during a situation a person can ask the other person, "How does this affect you?" I believe that empathy is a gift that is asked for with God and strengthened in each and every one of us. Practice being the other person once in a while, just to see how he or she may think of a certain situation. Empathy teaches us to love one another, as with it we can see how we are affecting other people around us.

Imagine how your words affect the person hearing them. Think about this for a second, and read that last sentence again. In other words, pretend to be the person you are talking to, and imagine how you would feel upon hearing your words. A person can practice this very easily. Just ask yourself something like, "How did I affect that person by being friendly and offering to help?"

Give Cheerfully

Think of how and what you can do for another person rather than what that person can do for you. Then apply how God wants you to be by reading his Bible and applying all his principles. Set the example for all people around you by putting to work all of what is in the Bible. God wants you to give without expecting or wanting anything in return. Yes, think about this a second. When God puts it on your heart to give to someone, give with all of your heart. Expect nothing in return. Be cheerful about it. "I have shewed you all things, how that so laboring ye ought to support the weak, and to remember the words of the Lord Jesus, how he said, It is more blessed to give than to receive" (Acts 20:35). What does this Bible verse mean to me? Well, it means that God has given me everything that I have. Therefore, I should be willing to give to someone in need when God asks me to give.

God gives us everything we have. Sometimes he will ask us (or other people may ask us) to give something that we have. Who are we to say no? Discretion is to be used, but many times God is testing us and wants us to give of ourselves and what we have. God wants us to serve him, and when we give without expecting something in return, we are being obedient to him. Since God gives us everything that we have, then we should give a little back when he asks us to.

When you need some help, ask for it. Should another person need help, give that person a hand without expecting anything in return. Yes, you heard that right. Do not expect anything in return. If you're asking why, then practice giving of yourself from your time, talents, or money to help you become a more giving person

I believe this to be one of God's principles to live by at all times. One of the barriers to acts of the heart is our giving the devil the stronghold of selfishness. This actually blinds a person, and he or she cannot see his or her own selfishness. The person is just thinking that he or she is in need of the the money or the object. My interpretation of the above Bible verse is that God has given you everything you have. So give some of what you have to the poor, because his blessings come upon those who give to others.

You can start giving to God by giving money or talent to churches or charities. Everyone has been gifted by God to do something: sewing, talking, organizing, doing physical labor, giving time, singing, playing an instrument, working in your profession (donate some of your business time), praying, washing dishes, cooking, baking—whatever you are good at, someone needs your help. Pray this prayer:

> Dear God, in the name of your Son, Jesus, please help me to overcome pride in this world. I thank you for allowing me to overcome pride within me, and I will practice giving of myself with my time, talents, and money when you ask me to. In faith I believe and know that only you can help me to overcome pride in my life. Amen.

Tithe to God

This is also related to tithing, which is giving to your church without expecting anything in return. In the book of Leviticus, chapter 27, verse 32, it states, "And concerning the tithe of the herd, or of the flock, even of whatsoever passeth under the rod, the tenth shall be holy unto the Lord."

Once we start giving, the Lord God will return unto us much more. We have to take the first step by making the choice to give. Remember, God is our Father. God gives each and every one of us something very special. This very special gift we are to share, and sometimes it is to share with others without asking for something in return. God has given you this special gift, so share it.

What is your special gift? Think about this for a second. What skill or ability do you have that comes very easily for you? Ask a friend or a pastor of your church what he thinks your gift might be. Ask God how you can share your gift. Pray, "Dear Heavenly Father, thank you so very much for this gift that you have given to me. I ask that you show me how I may serve you with this gift. I ask you this through your Son, Jesus. Show me your ways of love and giving. Thank you, Lord. Amen."

God wants you to draw closer to him by giving of your money and talents unto his kingdom. I give a minimum of one tenth of my pay to the church, and I have heard of others who give more than a tenth. The more that you give, the more you will be blessed by the Lord, our Father. Whatever you give, you will be given.

Sometimes God will take something away from you to bring you closer to him. He has done this to me. Once he took away from me a great sum of money. I will tell you how God got me closer to him in Chapter 3.

Pray for Others

Remember that whatever you say or do to other people is what you will receive back. So you want to do and say good things to other people as a daily habit. Practice good works when you catch yourself getting ready to say or do something mean to someone. Stop and say something nice instead, even if it is the opposite of what that person was trying to do to you. You do not have to hurt others just because they hurt you.

Break the trend and be a person of God. Pray for others that consistently hurt you. You are being empowered by God to pray for others in the name of Jesus. Pray: "Dear God, in the name of your Son, Jesus, please soften the heart of this person who is hurting me, and bring your peace into this person's life." Recognize that the person can only be helped by God and his ways, and that only through prayer can you help. Most of all, the person has to make a personal choice to pray for God's help.

Remember that praying for others is very powerful for you as a believer in God. This is an act of giving blessings and goodwill to others. Pray for their success. Do you understand this? By doing good for others, you will receive, in time, good things in return. Pray for the success of others, and you will also, in God's time, receive success. You pray for blessings for others, and you will receive blessings. You pray for safety for others, and you will receive safety. Please understand this, as this is very important. One way to receive God's love is to pray that God will show love to the people around you. Should this be the case, then you just have to pray that others receive God's love. Invite God into your heart right now—pray, "God, please come into my heart and show me your ways. Show me what you would like for me to know in your Bible as I read it. Thank you, Lord God, in the name of your Son, Jesus. Amen."

God wants you to get closer to him, and to do that, a person will focus on personal prayer by praying for others' needs. The power of prayer is so very powerful; it's the most powerful action a person can do on this earth. The prayer must be in love from your heart, for the good of others, and must be in the name of our Lord and Savior, Jesus. By saying these words, you are invoking very powerful spiritual works. You are invoking God's will and love. Just say, "In the name of our Lord and Savior, Jesus," and you are saying the most powerful words on this planet. Please understand this as I repeat what I just said in a different way: by speaking the words "in the name of our Lord and Savior, Jesus," in a loving manner, you have now planted a spiritual blessing of God, and by your faith, what you prayed for will become true.

Practice Forgiveness

The power of your good words to encourage others and your obedient service to God are both under the umbrella of becoming closer to God. Through your personal choice to learn about God, you are becoming closer to him. To become closer to God, a person has to forgive others for everything he or she thinks has been done wrong to him or her.

What does it mean to forgive? Well, it means to say in your heart that it is okay for what that person has done to you. Turn over what that person did to you to God. Just say, "God, in the name of your Son, Jesus, I give you this certain person to deal with as I forgive him or her for what he or she did. I ask you to bless this person with peace and love." We need God's help to forgive others. We cannot do this on our own, so we have to ask him to help us. Now pray this prayer out loud, thinking of the person who has been hurting you. Now pray for another person. Take your time, and as God reveals a name to you, pray for that person. Simple, isn't it? I am very proud of you for forgiving others who have hurt you. By forgiving these people and praying for them, you are releasing them to God.

The next step after forgiving them is to keep from bringing up the act by which they hurt you. Should it come up in conversation, say that you have forgiven them, and pray for them. Remember, you want to be forgiven by others, so therefore, you should forgive. To forgive means that you do not hold those actions against them. If they have broken the law, they still have to answer to the law. The law governs the land, and we all have to abide by the law. When we pass on from our life on earth, each and every one of us will answer to God for our actions.

Learn to Apologize

Have you been good to your fellow man? If you haven't, take a minute to think about what you may have done. Is there a way you can make up for what you have done to another person? Yes, there is. First of all, apologize and give back or undo what you have done to that person. After all, God wants you to grow closer to him by loving others.

Okay, I sense you are hesitating a little on this. Why do you think I know this? I know because I have been here at this spot before. What stops me from apologizing? A little doubt and just one other little itty bitty thing called ... pride. Pride is something that makes a person think he or she is better than another person, which is not true. In God's eyes, we are all equal. Yes, we are all equal. No one person is better than another. No matter how much money a person has, or what position a person holds in society, we are all equal in the eyes of God, although some of us may have more authority than someone else, empowered by the law or a job title.

This is the way we are to live in harmony with each other. When you do wrong to your fellow man, husband, wife, sister, brother, friend, or coworker, just admit it and apologize with your heart by meaning what you say. Pride has caused many fights, and without so much pride in each of us, we can prevent many of them.

Before you apologize to a person, allow God to intervene for you with his love by praying to him. Pray... "Dear heavenly Father, in the name of your Son, Jesus, I hereby bind anything and everything from the devil that may want to counter a loving conversation before, during, and after I apologize. Allow your words of love to flow from my lips and an abundance of loving forgiveness to be in the heart of the person whom I have wronged. Please be with me during this time and soften the heart of this person to be understanding and help us to be the best of friends. Father God, you are our strength and loving intercessor. God, I know whatever results come from the apology, your hand is all over the outcome. Through faith, I know you are always with me, and the end result is for my best well-being in the plans that you have for me. Amen." You may want to consider taking the words of this prayer with you and then pray with the person you are going to apologize to before you apologize to him or her. Now the two of you are in agreement in the name of Jesus and are both in the presence of God. Thank you, Jesus!

Okay, now go find a person whom you have wronged and apologize. Yes, get ready to go, and I will wait for you. Put a book mark on this page to keep your place, and you can continue on from here.

When you apologize, say the apology with love. Here, say this: "I am really sorry for what I did to you, and I would like to apologize with all of my heart. Please forgive me for what I've done. Is there anything I can do to make up for it?" Now, you can call this person, write this person, or simply tell him or her in person.

You can do this, I know you can. Is there someone you've wanted to talk to for a long time? Well, now is the time to get in touch with him or her and say you are sorry. Forgive that person if you think he or she provoked you to do something. You are preparing to get in touch with the person who is on your mind. Approach the conversation with love and understanding, and keep a cool head. If need be, just say that you are sorry.

Let's practice this. "I am sorry." Good, now try, "I apologize." Good! Now say it again (yes, out loud), "I am sorry. I apologize." Very good, now one last time: "I am sorry. I apologize." That was pretty easy, wasn't it? So now you are an expert. Put this book down right now, and go say you're sorry to someone you've offended. I will wait for you. Go on ...

Welcome back! Praise God for helping you to ask for forgiveness from that person and to say you're sorry.

Giving and Receiving

Empathy is directly related to giving and receiving. In the book of Galatians in the Bible, chapter 6, verses 7 and 8, you find God making these statements, "Be not deceived; God is not mocked: for whatsoever a man soweth, that shall he also reap. For he that soweth to his flesh shall of the flesh reap corruption; but he that soweth to the Spirit shall of the Spirit reap life everlasting."

These last two Bible verses combined together make for two of the strongest principles of God to live by. They are very, very important. The first says that whatever you give you will receive. So say, for example, that you want to be visited by other people at your home when you get older. That means you should go out and visit older people in their homes now, so you plant the seed of visiting other people, and your harvest is that they will come to visit you. In the meantime, you are giving other people a blessing of your time, presence, love, and words of encouragement. This is just an example and can be applied in many, many different ways.

Have Faith

What is faith? Faith is knowing that something is going to happen and speaking as though you have already received what you have asked God for in the name of his Son, Jesus. God answers the prayers of people who are faithful to him. This is a difficult term to talk about. My best guess is that prayers come to pass when all the right combinations of faith, prayer, your heart, your beliefs, the manner in which you talk to others, and your obedience to God are all working together. When all of these are working together, I believe that God will answer most prayers.

When you pray, it is okay to ask God for something and then thank him for what you are asking for. This, I believe, is speaking in faith. You are practicing believing that you have received what you just asked for and thanked God for. Here, let's practice a simple prayer. Speak this out loud, from your heart (this means that you really mean what you are saying):

> Dear heavenly Father, God, in the name of your Son, Jesus, I come to you with praise, honor, and thanksgiving. I pray that you will come into my heart and love me and show me all of your love. Thank you for coming into my heart and for showing me all of your ways. Thank you for helping me to understand your words in the Bible. Continue to help me thoroughly understand your words in the Bible, and I whole-heartedly thank you for this. Lovingly, your child in Christ, (insert your name).

Learn God's Word

God wants you to know that he wants you to read his Word—the Bible. God wants you to know that you should always honor him and not take any credit for what he has done for you and blessed you with. Everything that you have—your possessions, your mind, your body, your lungs, your hands, your talent, your abilities, your love, your family, the air that you breathe, life itself—you are to thank him for these and in expectation of your needs being met. When others thank you for giving of your time and talents, tell them that you are a servant of God, that God has given you this time for service, and they should thank God for your service and help to them. While you are serving God, be cheerful in his joy and love. By serving God in a church or a charity, give of yourself in joy and cheer. Read this Bible passage over and over until you really understand it: "If ye keep my commandments, ye shall abide in my love; even as I have kept my Father's commandments, and abide in his love. These things have I spoken unto you, that my joy might remain in you, and that your joy might be full" (John 15:10–11).

These verses tell me how a person can have joy in his or her life and keep it to its maximum. This is awesome. Some people may be looking to be happy and joyful. Invite the love of God into your heart, stop sinning, and become joyful. Applying all of God's principles makes a person happy in his or her heart and spirit. It gives that person a good feeling, as it does for me. People are always looking to be happy. So all a person has to do is make other people feel happy, and they, in turn, will feel happy. This makes sense, as it is in accordance with God's principle of reaping and sowing. God bless you and the way you give of your love to others.

God's commandment to love thy neighbor as thyself is very powerful. For many years, I thought that commandment was optional. I could choose to be jealous of my neighbor, envy him or her, or simply not like him or her. Well, I've got a little news for you. God's commandment really does mean to love your neighbor as yourself, and if I am jealous, envious, or hateful, then I am disobeying the commandment and committing a sin.

So how does a person keep from being jealous, envious, or simply hateful towards his or her neighbor? A person cannot do this without the help of God. We simply cannot do this on our own; we have to pray to God through his Son, Jesus. We are always being attacked with bad thoughts from the devil to not like someone or something. Although these bad thoughts are really not our own, we are still responsible for our words and actions. So we have to seek the help of our Lord and Savior, Jesus. Let's pray:

> Dear heavenly Father, in the name and shed blood of your Son, Jesus, I thank you in faith for allowing me to pray for, bless, and love my neighbor. Strengthen my prayer life in words that I speak verbally and in my mind, to love all people that come into my life, so that I speak life

> unto others, as all people are considered my neighbors. Thank you for the strength to be a good neighbor to all mankind. I ask these things in the precious name of your Son, Jesus. Amen.

God wants you to grow closer to him by repeating his verses from throughout the Bible and by learning his ways that are talked about in his Word. This is so very important. Please learn (and pray for others to learn) his ways. Remember the verses and reference numbers if you can. God will give you what you need to know in his verses for the particular time in your life.

The Bible is your guide to live by in life. Think of God and his ways in everything you do. Speak love and life unto others at all times. God's Word is the foundation on which you are to live, day in and day out. A foundation is the base on which you are to grow in knowledge, like a house is built on concrete, dug deep into the ground. The Word of God is also a foundation that is embedded deep into your heart and spirit. In Luke 6:47–49 it states:

> Whosoever cometh to me, and heareth my sayings, and doeth them, I will shew you to whom he is like: He is like a man which built an house, and digged deep, and laid the foundation on a rock: and when the flood arose, the stream beat vehemently upon that house, and could not shake it: for it was founded upon a rock. But he that heareth, and doeth not, is like a man that without a foundation built an house upon the earth; against which the stream did beat vehemently, and immediately it fell; and the ruin of that house was great.

One of the things I get out of these paragraphs is that, by doing God's bidding, we are building a great foundation on which to live. These are great tools to become Christ-like, to become like Jesus. I interpret the word *house* to represent a person's life—the way in which a person lives is his house. The Scripture passage gives us two examples, one that is good and strong, and one that is weak, without a good foundation. I think I would want to live in the house of God with a strong base and foundation of God's Word.

This is my reason for quoting his words and sayings throughout the chapters. His Word is final, and your interpretation of the Word should always be with love. The words and sayings mean different things to different people. Read the words with love, as they were intended from God. Dig a deep foundation that is strong on God's Word, act in his ways, change your heart to his ways of love by opening your heart to his love, and this is how you will become closer to God and fulfill your destiny. God wants you, and when you start loving him with all of your being, you will naturally get closer to him, and you will want to share this love with others, thus receiving his peace.

I encourage you to learn this as soon as you can, and live a full life as God intended. Break away from your old ways and follow God's ways. Use the power of your personal choice to follow God's ways right this very second. God wants you to pray for your loved ones. Pray that they become closer to God and for God to fill them with his love continuously and to sanctify them. Pray for God to bless them and to save them. God bless you and your growth to become closer to him in your daily lives. God bless you in your prayers for others. You will find that you will be praying several times each day and speaking to God all the time. To believe in faith is all you have to do.

Freedom from Sin

Sin is a way of life that is against God's laws. This is a tough one to describe. God has his laws, as in the Ten

Commandments. However, there are ways he wants us to live that will give us peace and joy in our hearts.

Throughout life, people may live in sin and not realize it. Say, for instance, a person grows up thinking it is okay to steal from other people. As an adult, this person is still going to think it is okay to steal. He or she grows up without feeling guilty for what he or she has done.

This is the way that sin works: once a sin becomes a habit, no guilt or remorse is part of the person's thinking. The problem comes about when a person does not get caught by society, or corrected at the time of the first offense. This is like a crack in a big rock; next thing you know, water gets into the crack, then it freezes and expands. Then it thaws, refreezes, expands, and the crack gets bigger.

Sin is the same way. It just gets bigger as people naturally want to do something bigger and better than the last time. Well, I have some sad news for people who sin. They always get caught, because the devil wants to destroy people. Many times, really dumb things are done because the devil tells people it is okay, or gives them a stupid reason to do something. We have all done things like this.

How does a person keep from doing dumb things? All a person has to do is ask God for guidance and wisdom, along with remaining sinless. Remember that if a person lives in sin for years and years, the person will not realize or understand that what he or she is doing is wrong. Either society will correct the person, or, if it is a hidden sin, God will correct it through people. People can act for God in ways of being servants to God. God can deliver a message through a person, and sometimes it can result in a person delivering prophetic words to the sinner.

Ask God to show you ways in which you may be sinning, and ask God to bring a person to show you, lovingly, how and why you are sinning. Ask God to show you how you are sinning, and stop doing the sin. Pray for deliverance from the sin and to have peace from the sin. When tempted to sin, ask God, in the name and shed blood of Jesus, to make the temptation leave you alone. Keep doing this until the thoughts are gone and do not return. Confess to others that you have sinned and that you have been healed and saved from the sin. Thank God for relieving you of the sin. Go make a telephone call to a pastor or preacher at a local church, and talk to him one-on-one.

Remember that the devil is the very best at deceiving people into thinking that the wrong that they are doing is in some way okay. Sin is not okay, and it is wrong. The only way people can help themselves is by knowing and accepting that what they are doing is wrong. Once this happens, they can recover. The devil puts out traps of pride and selfishness to keep people from realizing that they are wrong.

Many times, what people think and say to others are really the thoughts the devil is putting into their minds. These statements are not the real actions, motives, or even thoughts of what another person is being accused of. The person who accuses other people is usually the person guilty of the offense. Say, for instance, a person is accused of being greedy by a person of influence when an opportunity to make money is knocking. God's wisdom provides the opportunity, and the person of influence finds a reason (such as greed) not to go through with the money making opportunity. Because of the power of his influence, the opportunity to make money was hindered; therefore, the money is not earned and the opportunity wasted. No money is made through the God-given opportunity. The person of influence stopped the opportunity of the money-making proposition as the devil convinced him that there was a motive of greed,which in fact was not true.

All people know that greed is wrong. However, the influence of the devil kept a God-given opportunity from happening through control and the preconceived notion that greed was a motivating factor. The devil wins in this battle, but we all know that the devil has already lost the war through Jesus, the Son of God. By making ourselves open to change, and the thought that we may not always be right, we can make this a better world to live in with other people.

I find that when there is an argument, the two parties are usually right in their own way. It is a matter of trying to resolve the problem with the person who is the most justified, or of doing what God says is the right thing to do. A person cannot go wrong by doing what God wants done.

Praying ahead of time for God's blessing and direction is a positive way of approaching future events, and highly recommended. Many people seem to think it is easier to say no to something than to find ways to make things happen. Do you know anyone like this? If you do, pray for that person. He or she needs your help, as you recognize the problem of negative influences upon his or her life. Be a person who finds ways to make things happen in a positive way, for God's glory, and in service to him. God gives you experiences so that you may help others who are in the same situation.

Keep God First in Your Life

God wants you to come to him in good and bad times. Keep him first in your life. This means no habit, hobby, or addiction is to come before him. Read this statement again, as it is so very important. God is more important than any habit, hobby, or addiction that any person has. The person must love God more than any one of these. Just ask God to show you how to keep him first in your life and how to overcome the habit, hobby, or addiction. It is just that easy. He will show you how to overcome. Thank you, Jesus. These are some down-to-earth statements, supported by the first commandment: "Thou shalt have no other gods before me" (Exodus 20:3).

It is my opinion that addictive habits of pleasure or hobbies are ways that the devil keeps us busy from doing God's work, serving others, and growing in the love of God. Focusing our time, mind, and efforts into these areas keeps us from learning about God and getting to know him. In a sense, we are making a fictional god of our habits, addictions, or hobbies by worshipping the action or activity. God wants to be first in our lives.

What habits, addictions, or hobbies are consuming all of your time to keep you from learning about God and serving him? To break that way of life, all a person has to do is ask for God's help and stop the personal actions. In areas of difficulty, a professional counselor can help and should be consulted. The first step is to recognize that there is a problem, and then to keep the actions from becoming addictions. Wow, what a reality awakening! Let's turn this into a spiritual awakening. Hallelujah! Thank you, Jesus.

Follow God's Commandments

God wants us to live long, healthy, prosperous lives, without pain, and to be able to recognize and learn his principles and laws, to have his love, joy, peace, longsuffering, gentleness, goodness, and faith. These are the fruit of the Spirit, found in Galatians 5:22. God's laws are stated in the book of Exodus, chapter 20, verses 3–17:

1. Thou shalt have no other gods before me.

2. Thou shalt not make unto thee any graven image, or any likeness of any thing that is in heaven above, or that is in the earth beneath, or that is in the water under the earth. Thou shalt not bow down thyself to them, nor serve them: for I the LORD thy God am a jealous God, visiting the iniquity of the fathers upon the children unto the third and fourth generation of them that hate me; and shewing mercy unto thousands of them that love me, and keep my commandments.
3. Thou shalt not take the name of the LORD thy God in vain; for the LORD will not hold him guiltless that taketh his name in vain.
4. Remember the Sabbath day, to keep it holy. Six days shalt thou labour, and do all thy work: But the seventh day is the Sabbath of the LORD thy God: in it thou shalt not do any work, thou, nor thy son, nor thy daughter, thy manservant, nor thy maidservant, nor thy cattle, nor thy stranger that is within thy gates: For in six days the LORD made heaven and earth, the sea, and all that in them is, and rested the seventh day: wherefore the LORD blessed the Sabbath day, and hallowed it.
5. Honour thy father and thy mother: that thy days may be long upon the land which the LORD thy God giveth thee.
6. Thou shalt not kill.
7. Thou shalt not commit adultery.
8. Thou shalt not steal.
9. Thou shalt not bear false witness against thy neighbour.
10. Thou shalt not covet thy neighbour's house, thou shalt not covet thy neighbour's wife, nor his

> manservant, nor his maidservant, nor his ox, nor his ass, nor any thing that is thy neighbour's.

Here's a paraphrase of the commandments to make them easier to understand:

1. Do not worship any other gods.
2. Do not make any idols.
3. Do not misuse the name of God.
4. Keep the Sabbath (which is Sunday) holy.
5. Honor your mother and father.
6. Do not murder.
7. Do not commit adultery.
8. Do not steal.
9. Do not lie.
10. Do not covet (do not desire something that belongs to someone else).

Take a few minutes to spend with God by going somewhere quiet and thinking about each and every commandment. Go over each one, thinking of how you may have done wrong and how you can do better. Ask God, in the name of Jesus, to show you ways and to give you strength, and to keep you from breaking his laws. Let's pray:

> Dear heavenly father, in the name of your Son, Jesus, and through the shed blood of your Son, please forgive me for breaking your law(s). I cannot help myself, and I depend on you to show me how I have done wrong and to give me knowledge and strength to keep from breaking your law(s). Give me the words to speak the name of your Son, Jesus, when thoughts from Satan come into my mind to go against your laws. Only you can do this by my personal choice to serve you.

Father, please set me apart for your kingdom, bless me, illuminate the word of God unto my heart and mind, show me where I have been wrong, and please save me. Thank you, Lord, heavenly king, thank you. With all of your love, I pray and ask you these things, through faith in knowing and receiving. I believe you have given me what I have asked for.

Father, I know you are the God of peace. Please show me what to pray for in order to bind behaviors in myself and others. During times of disagreement, I pray for peace and harmony with others. Amen.

Chapter Two

WOULD YOU LIKE TO HAVE WISDOM?

WOULD YOU LIKE to have wisdom? If so, how do you get it? Where does it come from? How do I know when I have it? How do I recognize it? What is wisdom?

What is wisdom? I will tell you some answers that I have received and recognized for myself, through my own experiences. Wisdom is the knowledge that you are doing what God has commanded through his spiritual laws, and therefore, you know how to successfully apply his spiritual laws to receive peace, prosperity, and the fruit of the Spirit.

So how does a person get wisdom? First of all, a person should pray for wisdom by asking God, in the name of Jesus, to receive his wisdom. James 1:5 states, "If any of you lack wisdom, let him ask of God, that giveth to all men liberally, and upbraideth not; and it shall be given him."

Wisdom in Speech

Please understand this: whatever is said from a person's lips is very commanding and sets forth spiritual laws. As

Proverbs 18:21 says, "Death and life are in the power of the tongue: and they that love it shall eat the fruit thereof."

Speak words of life to yourself, your loved ones, and other people, as you will receive what you give by spiritual law. Luke 6:7 says, "Do not judge, and you will not be judged. Do not condemn and you will not be condemned. Forgive, and you will be forgiven. Give and it will be given to you. A good measure, pressed down, shaken together and running over, will be poured into your lap. For with the measure you use, it will be measured to you."

So you can see by the scriptures that what you give and how you give, by thinking or doing, is affecting your life as to how you receive. Two statements I hear a lot are: "you're killing me" and "you make me sick." To take this literally, one would think that every time he or she sees this person, the person is actually killing him or herself in some way or making him or herself sick.

I have found that changing my speech to always give life to myself and others is like learning to speak all over again. Try it: watch and listen to what you are saying. Speak love, encouragement, and hope to yourself, your children, and all people around you. What do you think happens to a person when you say in anger, "You're stupid"? That person will soon begin to believe what you say. Are you not speaking death upon that person? What if you were to say to a person, "You do not look very well; are you sick?" If you keep saying that to a person, that person will start feeling sickly. So words are powerful. Do not gossip about other people by putting them down. Speak of the good things that they do, and speak about a person in the way you would like him or her to be. Speaking the bad truth about a person does not help the person, as it only cements the situation as it is. Speak life in your words of encouragement unto the person by speaking how you would like him or her to be.

If a person is an alcoholic, speak as though the person were overcoming alcoholism, and speak words in faith that the person is no longer an alcoholic. For instance, "My brother in Christ is overcoming the challenges of alcohol and will no longer be drinking alcohol."

I believe that God puts people into our lives so that we can pray for them. Even when I am walking down the street or driving in my car, I am always praying for behavior in folks that I think is not appropriate. I pray for people who are in accidents or when I see an ambulance going somewhere.

Wisdom with Money

One of the examples of God's wisdom that was very pronounced to me I saw when I began tithing properly. Yes, tithing. Tithing means tenth. Leviticus chapter 27, verse 32 says, "And concerning the tithe of the herd, or of the flock, even of whatsoever passeth under the rod, the tenth shall be holy unto the Lord." Genesis 28:22 says, "And this stone, which I have set for a pillar, shall be God's house: and of all that thou shalt give me I will surely give the tenth unto thee."

Giving one-tenth of one's earnings back to God is giving cheerfully something that is really not ours, but a gift of our talent back to God. The other side of this is, in essence, robbing God of his tithes, as referenced in Malachi 3:8, which in my eyes now is considered to be a sin. "Will a man rob God? Yet ye have robbed me. But ye say, Wherein have we robbed thee? In tithes and offerings." Today there are different views on the percentage to give, and I prefer to give ten percent, as you will notice throughout these writings. Each person has to decide for his or herself what amount to give to God's kingdom. In the flesh or being human, the amount of money given could be considered like a type of personal, financial insurance, with God being the underwriter of the policy, utilizing spiritual principles and laws.

So, by the spiritual law of reaping and sowing, or harvesting what is planted, the spiritual law of giving first before one receives is applied here. A person gives one-tenth of his or her salary to God, and God, in turn, gives a person the wisdom in and protection of his or her finances. The wisdom of finances is learning to spend more thriftily and wisely by purchasing items that will last longer, with less maintenance. A person's money actually goes further by having God's wisdom and becoming more fruitful.

In order to receive wisdom and blessings of finances, a person, business, or organization has to give money first, before receiving in any abundance will occur. In science, it is said, "for every action there is a reaction." So give to a church the first ten percent of your earnings before all the deductions. Nowadays people can give by direct deposit from the company they work for to the church. The secret is to give regularly in order to receive from God regularly.

God loves a cheerful giver. A person is not to expect anything in return for giving to a church or any other entity. It is God's will to do with the money as he wills, as the church's ultimate mission is to bring God's people closer to him.

God expressed to me that tithing is a blessing of knowledge in knowing one of God's ways of doing things here on earth. It is a blessing to have this knowledge so as to be able to apply it to your finances in your life. It is also a gift from God to know that tithing is a gift. Giving to others lovingly, whether it is in finances or anything else, is considered a gift. Pray for this in the name of Jesus, the Son of God. All you have to say in prayer is, "Please Father God, in the name of your Son, Jesus, please give me the gift of giving with love from my heart. I want this so I may honor and glorify you. Allow me to serve you faithfully. Amen."

What a great gift to not have to be concerned about money when you know that God is now in charge of your finances. Consider charity as being a highly prized gift recognized by God. Charity comes from your heart, where God lives. 1 Corinthians 13:13 says, "And now abideth faith, hope, charity, these three; but the greatest of these is charity."1 Corinthians 14:1 goes on to say, "Follow after charity, and desire spiritual gifts, but rather that ye may prophesy."

In my opinion, it appears as though once a person has a charitable heart, God now opens the door for the person to receive other spiritual gifts to help build up the church. God also gives a person wisdom of where to invest for the future, how to spend, and how to be more thrifty, to be good stewards of his or her money. Once you start tithing, you turn your finances over to God, and they belong to him. Your bills and other necessary expenses for you and your family now belong to him, and you are representing him by how you live. God gives a new protection of your material items to last longer, along with guiding you on how to spend more wisely. Now a person's primary focus is on God, which is the main goal, and no longer on the material items, therefore making it easier to inherit the fruit of the Spirit.

This is actually a gift from God, knowing this about tithing. I wish I was taught this when I was growing up as a child. I am now just learning this, and I am almost 50 years old. This was a very important lesson for me as a father. I have now taught my son to tithe, and the importance of it, and I now pass this information on whenever I can. One thing to remember is that a person can pass this knowledge and wisdom down to other people; however, a person must make the personal decision to tithe. I am so thankful that

I have realized the wisdom of this gift as a father, because I know that my son's finances will be taken care of as long as he personally tithes.

I have done all that a father can do for a son. Instead of giving him financial support, I am showing him how to prosper with finances for himself. In other words, it is now in God's hands to show him how to take care of his own money by giving him the wisdom that he needs. I know he will be taken care of in finances. God is in control. My wife and I have always told our son that we are his parents; however, he has to answer ultimately to God. God is the Father and the Almighty.

People will recognize wisdom as they see for themselves that they are being fruitful. Proverbs 9:10 says, "The fear of the Lord is the beginning of wisdom." Let me throw an example your way. Say that a person gets into trouble with finances. This person then asks God for money. In reality, is money going to fall from the sky? Probably not. Is that person going to win the lottery? Probably not. If those people had God's wisdom, they probably would not have gotten into this problem. I can say this from personal experience, and laugh about it too.

To be truthful, when a person does not tithe a minimum of one-tenth, the person is robbing God of his tithes—the money that is due to God. It is a curse when a person does not tithe, as the money is not blessed. In the Bible, Malachi 3:8–10, it states:

> Will a man rob God? Yet ye have robbed me. But ye say, Wherein have we robbed thee? In tithes and offerings. Ye are cursed with a curse: for ye have robbed me, even this whole nation. Bring ye all the tithes into the storehouse, that there may be meat in mine house, and prove me now herewith, saith the Lord of hosts, if I will not open you

> the windows of heaven, and pour you out a blessing, that shall not be room enough to receive it.

Remember that God has given you all of your talents and abilities.

A person should tithe systematically with the first fruit of his pay, before buying anything else, and do it cheerfully. Blessing will then come systematically. Should a person tithe here and there, then the blessing will come here and there. Remember in Acts 20:35b it says, "It is more blessed to give than to receive." Pray while paying your bills, that your finances will be blessed by God, and be cheerful about paying your bills, praying that the people receiving the money will be blessed by it.

Once you tithe, all your money belongs to God in a sense, and he is in control, so the incoming and outgoing finances are blessed. When you recognize the blessing and thank God for it, this is a blessing in itself. God governs your finances and has his loving touch on them, once you tithe systematically. You will know this when you have developed the habit of tithing every time you receive income; you will instinctively think of giving money to God's work.

What I am talking about throughout this book is learning God's principles in stages, a little at a time. Learning in stages is how you, dear reader, will get close to God. So the first step is giving or tithing to God's work a percentage at a time, until you get to ten percent or above. A person may wish to start at one percent and build up over six months to get used to the giving and offering.

There is a stage of giving when a person wants to give to every charity and cannot decide which one to give to beyond the church. There is another stage when you know people in need of financial help around you, and you give them a little at times to help them out, but then comes a time that you stop giving. You might think this is cruel, but they are not going to learn God's principles of giving before they receive if you decide to give to them all the time. Instead, they will go from person to person, looking for pity and for someone to feel sorry for them. People like this go from person to person, repeating the same behavior over and over again. This behavior has to be broken, and they need to learn to help themselves. That is why nations become great nations: because they will help out the needy, and at the same time, help them to help themselves.

Do you happen to know someone who goes from one financial tragedy to another? I think tithing would help this person change and break this behavior, since what he or she is doing is not working. I have seen people doing the same things for over thirty years without being successful. This, to me, would mean that something needs to change.

I think an important principle of God's is for people to give even when they think that there is none to give. We get so wrapped up in what we are doing for ourselves that we neglect other people and their needs. Find a way to volunteer somewhere and give of your time. Give of your time, money, or talent while you are young, so that, should a need come about, God will provide people to give to you in your time of need.

Being part of a church body is awesome. People give of their time, talents, and finances throughout their lifetimes, and when it comes to a point that they are in need, they are provided for. It's sad when people go through an entire lifetime of not giving unto others, and then when they do need something, there is no one to give to them, because they do not know a whole lot of people.

When I was in the fifth grade, I started delivering newspapers on an Army Post here in Colorado Springs. I was always trying to figure out ways to make money. I would even go around and shovel snow for people during the winter, and when I needed some money to go see an afternoon matinee, I would go ask people with trash in their yard if I could pick it up for them for twenty five cents. A movie ticket back then cost thirty five cents, and then it went up to fifty cents. The Army Post, school, swimming pool, matinee, and commissary were all within a mile and a half. I got around most of the time by walking.

I would like to give you a personal example of why it is important for money to be blessed. To me, money is blessed when it is prayed over to do God's work, and a ten-percent portion of any money coming in should be given to God's work in some way.

Back in the late 1980s, my loving parents wanted to financially take care of their children, so they invested in a life insurance-type policy that would grow into more than a million dollars for each of us children when we were in our retirement years. This would have been 20 plus years from then. I have to admit that this was a very good idea. Each of us could contribute additional funds each month if we liked.

I remember our parents calling us all over one night for a family meeting. What a joyous event it was. Our parents loved us so much that they were thinking of our future and giving us this bounty of their love. Well, it so happened that during the mid-nineties the company came under investigation for fraud, and our funds were not growing like the agent had said they would. We were swindled. Wow, what a let down! All of us children had counted on this funding and did not really look out for ourselves, so that we could start contributing to our own retirement in some fashion.

When it comes to saving money, time is very important, for interest accumulates and compounds over the many years, and so on. This did not happen, so none of us received the million that we were promised, and on top of that, we did not prepare ourselves for retirement up to that time. I tell you this because I firmly believe and know that the money was not blessed. It was not blessed from my parents in that they did not tithe to God the Father first. They gave from their hearts, and very lovingly, but God did not bless the money.

When we received the money that did come out of the transaction, my wife and I did not tithe any of the money to God either. So the money was not blessed when it was given to us, and it was not blessed when we received it. So it was not blessed for God's work, and this is why I feel it did not grow like it was supposed to.

Wisdom may have steered this in a different direction. The concept was good: the money could have earned what it was supposed to, and it could have happened the way it was promised, but it was just with the wrong company. I cannot judge the company, but I think that somehow it was not blessed by God. Thinking back, we were given the opportunity by someone else's wisdom, which we thought to be accurate and in line with what we thought was right at the time. I did not see how God was a factor, as I was not taught to tithe as a child, or to contribute my first fruit of finances to God's work. I just did not understand. My eyes were blinded and covered by Satan's ways. This book is intended to uncover your eyes and open your heart to God's love for you, and his ways, principles, and laws.

Ask God for Wisdom

God is the best partner a person can have in finances and business, as he is the author of wisdom. A person may be the smartest person on planet earth, yet be without wisdom. Why? A person can only get wisdom from God. It is so easy to get wisdom. Just pray and ask for it. Matthew 7:7 says,

"Ask, and it shall be given you; seek, and ye shall find; knock and it shall be opened unto you." Also, in James 1:5 it says, "If any of you lack wisdom, let him ask of God, that giveth to all men liberally, and upbraideth not; and it shall be given him."

If a person asks for wisdom and it is not given, there is a problem—a reason for God not answering. If the request is of a selfish nature, it will probably not be answered. In James 4:3 the Bible says, "Ye ask, and receive not, because ye ask amiss, that ye may consume it upon your lusts."

In the year 2003, I was working by myself, building a house in the mountains of Colorado. During that time I was fasting for spiritual reasons. In reverence for God, I was going without food, drinking only water and liquids without sugar. During this time of fasting, God had put it onto my heart that I was selfish. I could not help but agree—God had showed me ways in which I was selfish. This opened my eyes to know how to better serve God the Father Almighty, and how to be more serving and giving of myself.

Wisdom in Relationships

An important part of wisdom is the act of forgiving. What exactly is forgiving? Forgiving is the act of speaking, feeling, and accepting that what a person has done to you is okay, as God is the spiritual Father of the person who has done the wrong to you. We are to release the act of wrong a person has done and ask God to take care of it. We are not to take the law into our own hands.

Sometimes it is necessary to bring the authorities into play. Other times we are to turn away from the acts that are being brought against us. We are to act in love toward one another, even if we are being cursed. One of God's laws is in the last part of Luke 6:37, which says, "Forgive, and ye shall be forgiven." Forgiveness and love are directly connected to each other. Leviticus 19:18 states, "Thou shalt not avenge, nor bear any grudge against the children of thy people, but thou shalt love thy neighbor as thyself: I am the Lord." I have been in many situations where I found it very difficult to forgive, so I know that, only being one person, I have learned to allow pride to step aside and to ask God through his Son, Jesus, to help me to forgive this person and the acts done against me.

I know that I cannot do many things in life without asking for God's help. I now know that pride is a hindrance to my spiritual growth. At times I even ask God, "Dear Heavenly Father, in the name of your Son, Jesus, the Christ, please allow pride to leave me so that I may grow in the manner in which you want me to grow. Thank you, Lord. Amen." Remember, you have a spiritual power on earth in actually saying the name of Jesus in your prayer.

People should forgive all wrongs they feel have been done to them throughout their lives. This includes as a baby, a child, a youth, an adult, and every day when occurrences happen to them. Learn to forgive instantly. If you have done a wrong to someone, ask that person's forgiveness. Many times a person can visualize asking a person to forgive him or her for what he or she has done before even asking that person to forgive him to her. Then, in faith, he or she asks that person to forgive him or her for what was done. A person shows great character in asking forgiveness for a wrong which he or she has done.

The next big step is to correct the wrong to the satisfaction of the person wronged. So go on and ask the person, "What can I do to right the wrong that I have done to you?" Then be prepared to work out something that is reasonable to both parties. Remember to act in love during this process.

When Jesus died on the cross, a great spiritual event took place for each and every person here on earth. He died for each and every one of the sins that we have committed. Yes, he did. So now all we have to do is to ask God, through his Son, to forgive us for what we have done, and God will forgive us. Even though our sins are forgiven, we still have to ask God to forgive us. Once we do this, all we have to do is change the ways in which we have been sinning. The sin that we had committed is a weakness until we find strength through Jesus to overcome it. 2 Corinthians 12: 9 says, “And he said unto me, My grace is sufficient for thee: for my strength is made perfect in weakness.”

A person could interpret this to mean that through God’s grace unto a person, a sin can be overcome in our weakness, and when this happens, it is then the strength to overcome that is made perfect in God’s eyes. Many times people are inflicted with some type of sickness that was pronounced when the person had committed a sin. Because the sin was not recognized as a sin, the person did not ask God for forgiveness. Therefore the sickness just lingered. We have the power to personally ask for forgiveness for the sins we have committed. However, we must forgive others in order for us to be forgiven. Luke 6:37b says, “Forgive and ye shall be forgiven.” Because of the forgiveness, love prevails, heals, and surrounds us.

A couple of years ago, I was sitting in a meeting with a dozen Christian brothers from the Colorado Springs Chapter of Full Gospel Business Men’s Fellowship International. It was a cold, winter, Saturday morning, and we were sitting in a U-shaped formation in the meeting room. As I was relatively new to the group, I was in a learning phase (which I am still in). One of the gentlemen across from me had asked a question. He said, “How come when we pray for people, they are not always healed?” After I heard the question, I said to myself, *This is going to be a good answer, and I am very anxious to hear it.* As I sat there, I did not realize that I was in a time warp, where time slowed down for me, like it has done in the past. I was waiting for someone to stand up to answer, and it seemed like forever. All of a sudden, I felt as though I had the answer, but I did not know what it was. As I stood up out of my chair to go to the microphone, I sensed a strong push—a push with strength and power. I walked over to the microphone, and the Holy Spirit consumed me so that I was speaking, but did not really know what I was saying. I do remember saying that people are not healed because of forgiveness, and that they should pray for forgiveness before they are healed. Forgiveness was the basis for my answer to his question.

The gentleman that had asked the question did not know that I was consumed by the Holy Spirit until I told him about 6 months later, in which he received a confirmation. This was a very powerful experience for me as a servant of God. I love you, Lord God, and thank you for using me to help edify the church body.

So healing, I think, is hindered when a person does not pray and ask God for forgiveness for past sins. To help you understand what sins to ask forgiveness for, dear reader, please pray this prayer:

> Lord God, in the name of your Son, Jesus, please reveal to me the sins I have committed that I need to ask forgiveness for. I open my mind to you, and with your help, I pray that you will now forgive me for these sins. As the sins comes to my mind, one at a time, please forgive me for them. Lord God, please reveal to me who I am to forgive that I have not forgiven. With your help, give me the words to verbally say that I forgive them, and to tell them verbally that I have forgiven them. If they have

> already asked me for forgiveness and I said no, give me the strength to contact them and tell them that I forgive them, and to ask them to please forgive me for not forgiving them earlier. Amen.

Ask God to reveal to your heart how he would like you to pray for other people. Pray this prayer:

> Dear God, thank you for your Son, Jesus. Through your Son, Jesus, I thank you for wisdom and understanding of your principles and laws in the Bible and for blessing my income and outgoing finances. Thank you for the people who have blessed me with these finances to take care of and meet the needs of my family. Open the eyes of my heart to see your ways, and help me to help other people, to be able to explain to them so the eyes of their hearts are opened to understand you and your ways, Lord God. Amen.

The Wisdom of God's Word

Wisdom is contained in the Bible, as it is God's Word. There are different parts of the Bible that I will share with you, dear reader, which are God's principles and laws to live by. Okay, you might say, "I read the Bible." Well, a person just has to go one step further and start applying it. Okay, what are some ways a person can apply the Bible to life to receive wisdom? Obeying the Ten Commandments is a priority, but there is more. Yes, there is more. There are spiritual laws in which a person receives what he or she plants through a harvest. What you plant is what you will harvest, right? Galatians 6:7 says, "Be not deceived; God is not mocked: for whatsoever a man soweth, that shall he also reap." This to me is one of the most powerful verses that we can apply in our daily life.

The many biblical scriptures quoted throughout these chapters are very powerful as they are words provided by God. Each of you will get out of each Scripture quote a personalized understanding of the quote regarding what God wants you to know at the specific time that you read it. It is the Holy Spirit who is giving you the life-giving food of the Word that you need.

Reading God's words in the Bible will give you answers as to how you are to act and why God sometimes does things the way he does. For instance, once he corrected me as I was going in the wrong direction by buying tax lien certificates, wanting to acquire other people's hard-earned and paid-for land. He corrected me by having the very same thing done to me, to teach me a lesson and show me that his principles are the way of the world. He took away a house that I had built by selling it to someone else. On top of that, I lost all the equity of the higher appraised value versus the loan repayment amount, about $50,000. The buyers instantly had this money in their pockets at the time they bought it. So I am to be careful with what I say and what I do.

The biblical passage that gives me comfort is in the book of Proverbs, chapter 3, verses 11–12. Before you read it, visualize and think for a few minutes about the biggest hurt and pain that you have ever had in your life, and then read these comforting sentences. Also, remember and know that God has allowed these things to happen to correct you, or to get your attention, and maybe even to use you as his strength to help others in the same circumstances to be as strong as you are, and to prevent further occurrences like what has happened to you. Here are his comforting words: "My son, despise not the chastening of the Lord; neither be weary of his correction: For whom the Lord loveth he correcteth; even as a father the son in whom he delighteth" (Prov. 3:11–12).

As a child of God, you might need to be corrected once in a while. You, dear reader, may have been corrected like I was. How did you choose to make right the correction, and how did you deal with it? I chose to go to God, my Father, and ask him to show me why I did wrong and how to live in the future and how to make myself a better person through understanding more of his ways.

Here are some other Scripture quotes that concern wisdom. This one is from Proverbs 7:4: "Say unto wisdom, Thou art my sister; and call understanding thy kinswoman."

What I get out of this scripture is that we are to know that wisdom is a spiritual entity like a sister, and understanding is also a spiritual entity, like a female blood relationship in the spiritual realm.

Proverbs 9:10–11 says, "The fear of the Lord is the beginning of wisdom: and the knowledge of the holy is understanding. For by me thy days shall be multiplied, and the years of thy life shall be increased."

Wow, what powerful passages! These three sentences tell a person what is needed to gain wisdom, what understanding is, and that by knowing God, a person's days on earth will be longer. The combination of understanding God's ways with wisdom is a very powerful tool for Christians to enable them to live in Christ-like behavior. To simplify this statement would be to live the way God wants us to through his verses in the bible.

Proverbs 3:13–18 says:

> Happy is the man that findeth wisdom, and the man that getteth understanding. For the merchandise of it is better than the merchandise of silver, and the gain thereof than fine gold. She is more precious than rubies: and all the things thou canst desire are not to be compared unto

> her. Length of days is in her right hand; and in her left hand riches and honour. Her ways are ways of pleasantness, and all her paths are peace. She is a tree of life to them that lay hold upon her: and happy is every one that retaineth her.

Once people start understanding different things going on in their lives according to God's ways, they will become happier. Answers are now coming unto their minds and hearts about the actual ways of God and how the ways of mankind need to be changed to God's ways.

Chapter Three

HOW GOD GOT ME CLOSER TO HIM

IN TODAY'S WORLD, different challenges come upon people during special times in their lives. Often times we are challenged to a limit that God knows we can handle, to build us up for the next spiritual level he wants us to achieve. I would like to share with you a personal, family experience that has brought me to a spiritual level that is very close to God. The story has life lessons that can be learned by others. We are to consider challenges to be learning experiences and seek out God during these times, seeking his love for us and how to serve him with the gifts that he has given to us.

God has gotten me closer to him through my weakness. The Bible states that our weaknesses shall become our strengths. Look at 2 Corinthians 12:10, which states, "Therefore I take pleasure in infirmities, in reproaches, in necessities, in persecutions, in distresses for Christ's sake: for when I am weak, then am I strong."

What was my weakness? It was money; yes, it was money. Maybe you think you also have this weakness.

Listen to your heart while you read about how God touched me, and you will learn a lesson without going through the trials and tribulations I experienced. God has a way of getting your attention; sometimes it may be little things, and sometimes it takes a person really messing up, like me. Here is my testimony, with some personal background information:

During the years of 1977 through 1983, I was serving our country in the United States Air Force as an electrician. My last tour of duty was overseas, in the beautiful country of England. While my wife, Rose, and I were living in England, enjoying the green countryside and fresh vegetables, I decided that I wanted to become a civilian and a licensed electrician in the state of Colorado. I chose Colorado, because Rose and I grew up there and considered it home.

So off we went to Colorado Springs. I started working full-time for an electric company, and I also worked part-time on many weekends to help pay off the house that we were living in. My goal was to pay off the house ahead of schedule, to save on payments of 10 or more years. Within a couple of years, I was working for the federal government as an electrician, and I continued to work weekends to pay off the house. I was in control of when the house was going to be paid off. I was determined to do this: it was my goal.

Rose and I wanted to become members of a church and to be able to receive Holy Communion, which is to receive the sacrament of the body and blood of Jesus. We were married in Colorado Springs, in a church called Immanuel Lutheran Church, just across the street from where Rose was born in St. Francis Hospital. We decided to become members there (what a coincidence, huh?). A seed was planted there for us when we married there in November of 1976. Many good experiences have occurred in our marriage and through our church, and there are many more to come. Thank you, Lord God, for this blessing of marriage and for the church members, as I love them all as brothers and sisters in Christ. It is just a great feeling to know that I have an extended family of brothers and sisters in Christ who love God as much as I do.

This is what church is about, growing in God's love and sharing his experiences with one another. My favorite part is being in the congregation when a child of God is baptized. This is so moving for me—seeing, praying, and experiencing the Holy Spirit tingle up and down the back of my legs and spine with goose bumps while a new child of God is entering his kingdom. The goose bumps, I now realize, are really a reflection of the presence of the love of God, and the fact that his hand is taking care of the situation. So whenever I see or witness love, goose bumps will appear on the backs of my legs and back. This is a very powerful experience.

This is how I am now; however, I was not this close to God during the beginning years of our church-going. For about 15 years I was the type of person who would find an excuse, like cleaning the garage or my car, to keep from going to church. My wife and (after 1989) my son would go to church without me. Ask yourself if you find excuses with your time to not go to church. If you find excuses not to go, please pray in the name of Jesus and ask God to give you the strength to overcome these thoughts and excuses which are keeping you away from learning about God.

Let's pray:

> Dear heavenly father, in the name of your Son, Jesus, please give me the time in my schedule to find ways to read your Bible and go to one of your churches every week, and more than once a week should you wish. Give

> me the boldness to become involved within the church. Show me the church that you want me to grow in. Thank you, Lord, for loving me so much and opening my eyes to all of your love. Amen.

Sometimes I would go to church, though, as I always had a rewarding spiritual growth experience. I would go every Easter and every Christmas. This was a sure thing for our family. I did not know until several years later that my wife was praying for me, as it saddened her to be going to church without me. Before Ryan was born, she would sit alone. I was finding all the different excuses not to go. This was my justification for staying busy. Now I know that the dark world of Satan wants to keep us busy doing other things so that we keep from growing in the Word of God. Now I find excuses to go, and going to church every week is part of my life so that I can be fed with the Word of God and see my sisters and brothers in Christ.

One significant thing that happened to me was the promise we made to God when our son, Ryan, was baptized. I made a promise to God during the baptism that I, as a father, would be responsible to lead our son into a spiritual path. This touched my heart, as I feel I am a responsible person. So Rose and I decided to give up our family vacations throughout the years so that we could send Ryan to a private, Christian school. I was learning then to sacrifice as a father to pay the tuition. God opened my eyes as to how selfish I was in my different ways then, and I continue to grow even today in being more giving.

I have also learned that our son has taught me many things in life about being a better person than I have been, even while I am also being a mentor to him by setting the best example I can as a father. This leads into many aspects of being a role model. I have to be what I expect him to be.

As a role model, I took on roles within the church leadership to set an example for him.

One of the roles I took was Boy Scout leader. When Ryan was young, I had asked him if he wanted to join Boy Scouts and if he wanted me to be a leader, and he said yes. Because I had been a Boy Scout when I was young and had learned a lot from the scouting program, I was prepared to be an adult leader within the organization at our church. I grew more and learned more than I thought I would. When a person volunteers to help out in an organization, one cannot help but learn and grow.

I encourage everyone to volunteer and get out of their comfort zone to help others. While you help others, you are growing yourself. Step out and do something different to help others. All a person has to do is give his or her best effort, with some of his or her time to make this a better world.

Another way I stepped up was to volunteer to be an usher for the church. This was difficult for me at first, as at the time I had a fear of people. God helped me and nurtured me with this. I boldly state that I volunteered; however, I have to actually thank God for using the boldness and love of a head usher at the time in calling me to volunteer. The first time he called and asked me to usher, I made an excuse that I was busy or something. I did not expect him to call back. Guess what? He did call back a week or so later, and I really did not know who he was at the time, only that he was asking me to volunteer to help usher one Sunday. I came up with another excuse not to usher for the church. *Okay,* I thought, *I got out of this one, and he won't be calling back*. How wrong I was, and I sure am glad to this day that he persevered in calling me. Thank you, Bill Gernand, for being a good servant of God. God bless you; this service to God has impacted my life immensely.

When he called back again, I gave in (out of feelings of guilt, for some reason) and said I would help out and usher one Sunday. Next thing I knew, I was on a regular schedule to usher. Thank you, Lord, for this service that I was to provide. This service led to me to become an elder within the church body and head elder for the church. I have many stories about the ways in which God has acted through me during this tenure, which I would like to share with you at a later time.

Anyway, I became an active leader within the church in order to set an example of leadership for our son. I felt this was very important for his growth, as I believe that I have a responsibility to Ryan to continuously set a good example by being a leader within our community and nation.

Rose and I have volunteered in other groups also, as Rose was the vice president, and then president, of the Parent Teachers League for the school for many years, all the time setting an example of leadership for our son. She is a great coordinator of volunteers, and I am very thankful for her. I encourage you to volunteer for different things and watch yourself grow. I say this with all of God's love for you: step out and grow. God is with you; he loves you very much. Step out in faith to new things and grow in the name of our Lord and Savior, Jesus.

Pray the Lord's Prayer and then the next prayer, saying both of them out loud. The Lord's Prayer is found in the book of Matthew, chapter 6, verses 9–13:

> Our Father which art in heaven, Hallowed be thy name. Thy kingdom come, Thy will be done in earth, as it is in heaven. Give us this day our daily bread. And forgive us our debts, as we forgive our debtors. And lead us not into temptation, but deliver us from evil: For thine is the kingdom, and the power, and the glory, for ever. Amen.

Memorize this prayer and pray it several times daily, and whenever God puts it onto your heart to pray his prayer:

> Dear Heavenly Father, in the name of your precious Son, Jesus, thank you for making me a bold person to volunteer to help others when you put it upon my heart to serve you. Strengthen me and protect me during this time, and throughout my life. Show me in my mind, heart, and spirit all the reasons to help others. When reasons of doubt come upon my mind to find ways not to help, I pray that you will remove the doubting thoughts and strengthen me to find ways to help others in the name of our Lord and Savior, Jesus. Thank you for enabling me to serve you with all of your love. I honor you and praise you, Lord God. Amen.

Whenever you pray, pray with love from all of your heart, mind, body, and soul, to project that love from within, into the atmosphere, and unto God.

Just before I became the head elder for our church, I entered into a financial transaction that resulted in the theft of money from Rose and me. This had a significant impact on our finances and took up a lot of my time. This whole transaction had become a spiritual battle ground for us. Ephesians 6:12–13: "For we wrestle not against flesh and blood, but against principalities, against powers, against the rulers of the darkness of this world, against spiritual wickedness in high places. Wherefore take unto you the whole armour of God, that ye may be able to withstand in the evil day, and having done all, to stand."

Reading this passage will allow a person to understand how this world really works, and how to fight against the bad things in this world. Continue reading the verses following 12 and 13, as they will give you the weapons for your personal battle and an understanding of how to protect yourself and others in your prayers, and to tell others how they can protect themselves.

When reading the Bible, always pray to God first, asking him to allow you to understand what is being said unto your mind and into your heart. The key to understanding God is just to understand that he is love and wants you to be more loving to people around you. Remembering one of the greatest commandments, in Matthew 19:19, Jesus says, “Thou shalt love thy neighbor as thyself.”

My interpretation of this means you are to love all the people around you as if they are your neighbors. I once thought this only means the person living next to you, which I have since changed to everyone on earth.

The spiritual battle my wife and I were opposing was theft and deception. I had fallen into a trap, and 75% of a construction loan was stolen. Consequently, I had to build a house in the mountains with the remaining money, about 25% of the total amount loaned to us. This was a very minimal amount, and I had to take money out of the equity in the house we were living in to finish building the house that I was now the general contractor for. The lending institution was also deceptive to me, telling me to continue building when the money ran out, even though they knew all along that they were not going to give me any more money beyond the amount that was in the loan. This caused mechanics liens to be filed onto the property.

We went through many different phases of emotions to accomplish the building of the house. I did most of the work myself after the money ran out from the construction loan. This was a major stress on me, as I did not know how to do the plumbing, the laying of floor ceramic tile, building closet shelves, installing walls, and installing cabinets. Most of this I had to learn how to do on my own. Then friends of ours, Rocky and Susan Rockefellow, and their son, Roger, came to our rescue by installing the plumbing fixtures, laying carpet, doing some texturing, and installing kitchen cabinets and counter tops. Thank you, Lord, for these blessed friends of ours.

There was also a lot of financial stress on me, as the lending institution was charging daily interest on the loan, adding up to about $2,300 per month. I could not pay this and make a living and stay afloat with our other expenses at the same time. I will never forget this nightmare of dealing with mortgage companies, lending institutions (such as credit unions), deceptive general contractors, lawyers, subcontractors, and people in general. I cannot describe everything that happened; this is a book in itself, which I plan to write in the near future. What my family and I went through would make a good movie for people to learn a lesson from.

One of the major lessons I have learned is that when people are going through an unpleasant experience, unless I have gone through it myself, I do not know what they are really going through. This, to me, was a very traumatic experience. So the lesson is that I should try to get involved in some way to help people out with problems that they may have, even if it's just asking if there's something I can do for them and being persistent. By asking more than once, saying, "There must be something that I can do," and by putting myself in their shoes, I should be able to come up with some way to help. Pride, yes, pride kept me from asking for help at times, and even when someone did offer to help, I did not take that person up on it if he or she was not persistent.

In conclusion, how God used this situation to bring me closer to him can be addressed in several ways. First, I had been buying tax lien certificates at the county tax lien sales and had actually acquired a piece of property from someone who did not pay the taxes on the property. Even though the process through which I acquired the property was legal, it was not the right thing to do. So the lesson I learned is that even though some ways of acquiring money are legal in today's world, it does not make them right. Please read this last sentence again and understand it. Just because some laws make things legal to do, that does not make them right in the eyes of God. Remember, God is love, and in some cases, if not all, if laws are not acting upon in order to love thy neighbor as thyself, then God is not happy. The real gift in God's eyes is to give first, and then you will receive; this is a spiritual principle and law. Acts 20:35b says, "It is more blessed to give than to receive."

The world is structured so that we earn everything we receive. Well, in God's eyes, whatever we give we shall receive, and have abundance of. It is just the opposite. We are to give unselfishly, without expecting anything in return. If we give food to the poor, then we will be blessed with food in abundance; if we give unselfish labor, then we will receive labor. If we give love to our neighbors, then we will receive love. Do you get the picture?

One of the other lessons I learned is that I did not give free labor to anyone, and I always charged some type of fee for any electrical work I did for them. I figured this was a business, and I should treat it like that. By not giving free labor to people throughout the years, no one really offered free labor to help us build an entire house. Okay, I learned a lesson here.

Also, I learned that by giving of myself in money or labor, I was also learning how to receive things people were willing to give to me. I was able to accept the offering of love without my pride getting in the way and saying no to the offering. I learned how people are so caught up with their own lives that they do not wish to help others in need. I used to be one of those people, I have to sadly say. So, if you expect people to do things for you just because you are a good person, forget it. You have to be a good person by giving to your brothers and sisters when they are in need, not just when you are ready to give or when you think you may have the time or money.

Here's another lesson learned: since we were having financial trouble because of money being stolen from us, I had to address whether or not I was robbing God of money that belonged to him. I now understand that I was indeed robbing God of his money, and I share that with you, dear reader, to guide you from making the same mistake. What do I really mean by this? God has given us all gifts and talents, so we are to give those gifts and talents to others at times, for no charge, and when we do receive money, we are to give a minimum of one tenth to his work. This can be to a church. Give cheerfully!

One day, at a Full Gospel Business Men's meeting, I shared that my family and I were in financial distress. This was hard for me to do, and I was looking for some kind of help. The president of the chapter, a retired pastor, lovingly put his hands on my shoulders and said, "Robin, are you tithing properly?" I had to reply that no, I was not tithing properly. The lesson I learned here was that I was the source of my own problems with money. I was not giving to God's work through tithing. If I had been giving first, then by the spiritual law of "you shall reap what you sow," I would not have gotten into this mess.

Tithing means a tenth. So I started right away, giving to God's work through our church by having funds electronically taken out of my paycheck. The money is the first fruit, so I give first and the best. The rest is for me to spend.

Well, I was giving because I was scared, and I later learned that this is not the right attitude. I am to give lovingly because I love God and his work. It took several months to learn this, as I was quite scared by the way God had gotten my attention. I felt as though I was being disciplined by my father, which I was. God turned his head and let the dark side of the world in to steal money from me. One way that I opened the door to theft from my family and me was by taking things that did not belong to me. Because of this I was taken from.

This is a most valuable lesson for people to learn. Please understand this. What we do opens doors to what we receive. We reap what we sow. Whatever we plant, we harvest. If what we do is bad, then we receive bad things. If we do good things, then we will receive good things.

There were some other lessons that I learned. Since we have talked about how what you give is what you receive, I can relate two experiences in which I had legally taken something away from someone. The first instance was the purchasing of the tax lien certificates. The second was when we bid on a car being auctioned off after its being repossessed. The car we bought was only a couple of years old, and the lady had to pay the difference, which our bid did not cover. I felt bad at the time, but we did not have a lot of money, and it was legal. I did not pay her any money, for the difference of the auctioned price, and I was not tithing.

When I took these things away from someone else legally, I set up circumstances in the spiritual realm which led to my being legally taken from. In my case, it was a house that I had built. So the point I am trying to make is that the circumstances I had set up in the past by my actions set up the circumstances of the present.

This is kind of scary and makes a person think about what actions he or she is taking today to set up future events. If the action does not feel right, even though it is legal, watch out. God and his principles prevail. I know, as I found out the hard way. You do not have to learn this way, as I did. You can learn from my mistakes, instead of making them yourself.

We deal with money and finances every day. It should be blessed through following God's principles in giving and receiving. As stated in Leviticus 27:32, "And concerning the tithe of the herd, or of the flock, even of whatsoever passeth under the rod, the tenth shall be holy unto the Lord."

By being holy, the tithe can be prayed for by you, that God would bless it to serve him and to bless the people and company. When you receive, bless it by saying thank you and by tithing a tenth or more to God's work.

Chapter Four

TODAY'S CHALLENGES FOR YOU

ONE OF THE ways that God will get you closer to him is by challenging you. By challenging you, I mean he will have you doing different things for him by helping others. When you help other people with the motive only of helping them, you are honoring God. However, if a person helps someone to get noticed—by getting an honorable mention of your name in a newspaper or on the job to impress the boss—by donating food, service, or money, this is not really giving and helping someone. As a living human being and a child of God, you will learn to help others without being asked to help them. Sometimes, you will be asked to help someone without even expecting to be thanked by the person you are helping. You are serving your loving God by helping those who need help.

The Privilege of Helping Others

I am about to share with you a very important concept. I would like for you to think on this a little, to understand the basis for what I am going to tell you. Remember, our ways are not God's ways, so in order to understand how God wants us to live, we have to listen to other people telling us what they've learned and also read in the Bible.

Okay, are you ready? I think you are ready to hear this: "It is a privilege to help someone." Say that to yourself one more time. "It is a privilege to help someone." You might ask yourself, *Why is it a privilege to help someone when I can be doing something for myself today?* The opportunity to help others never comes when you want to help people, but when they need help during their time of need.

Remember, it is a privilege and an honor to help someone, because they thought enough of you to ask you for help, or because you simply offered to help someone in his or her time of need. How wonderful would this be, if everyone was helping one another? This is why it is so wonderful to help others with joy and a smile. When people ask you for help, look on it as an honor and a great opportunity to give them a helping hand. It is better to give than to receive. If you need help some day, you can count on someone helping you. Whatever you plant, you will harvest.

This applies to helping others. By helping others, you are setting the example as a leader of helping people, and the people that see you helping your neighbors will then be inspired to help others also. So go ahead and be the leader and set the example of helping others. Should it not be the exact time to help, you are to make the time at that very moment, as the time may not ever come again, so that you can show that person how much God loves them by being God's representative of love and charity through your help and services. So stop and make the time, and provide your services, time, talents, or money, as the situation presents itself.

I would like to share with you an experience that happened to me a couple of years ago, during the time that we were building the house in the mountains, which I will remember for a long time. One evening I received a phone call, while at home, from a person who had been referred to me for some electrical work. I felt honored that the referring person had thought enough of my work to refer me to some friends of his. So I made an appointment with the gentleman to see how I could help him.

I went over to his house, he introduced me to his wife, and we proceeded downstairs to an unfinished basement. He explained what he wanted to do, and I explained the different electrical codes and what I could do within the rules. He wanted me to put some lighting in the ceiling that I did not quite agree with, as I did not think it would give enough lighting for the area. I explained how things would work out during the process so that I could help him with his electrical installation. I told him how much the materials would cost. He was about four to five weeks away from installing the electrical wiring, and I really did not think that he would call me back.

Well, he did call me back, and we set up an appointment to do the work. When I got there, we started installing the wiring. I just did not understand why I was there, as I just did not feel right, so I just came out and asked him, "Why am I here?" Now, is this not an odd statement? Normally, you tell someone you are going to do some work for him or her, and you just go and do it to the best of your ability, then move on to the next job. But this was not an ordinary job, and I just had to know why I was there.

He told me that he had prayed for someone to help him with the electrical portion of the job. He went on to say that he did not pray for a particular person, but just prayed for some help. This made a lot of sense to me, as I knew I had to be there as if I were called by a higher power. As a servant of God, one needs to respond when told what to do. I did feel as though I had done this by going to work for this person. I did not feel comfortable until I learned and understood the reason why I was really there. God wants you to be his servant and just do what he asks, and afterward you will understand why he wanted you at a certain place. Just do his work by faith, with joy and confidence. Do not question, doubt, or refuse your service to him. Should you feel any negative thoughts, just bind them instantly in the name of Jesus, sending them away, and continue on to complete the task that God has for you.

Well, as we were working along in his basement, a thought came to my mind that his prayer must be pretty powerful for me to be there when I did not feel quite right about being there. So curiosity got the best of me, and I had to ask him how he prays. I did; I asked him just that. He said that he is not a person to ask for things, and he has always thanked God for everything that he has been blessed with. He is a thankful type of person.

Boy, oh boy, did this scare me. I thought to myself, *He has been thanking God for almost thirty years* (he was probably in his mid to late thirties in age) *and now all of a sudden he asks for some help and is led to call me. I'd better do what he wants and more, so that I can please God.*

So now I knew why I was there. The big question was out of the way. What a relief to get an upfront, honest, Christian answer. I was sure motivated then. Chris had been unselfishly praying all these years, and probably praying for others as well. It was his turn to receive something from God in the form of human favor, which was my labor, talent, and knowledge, as well as presence of mind, body, and spirit. God bless you, Chris, for this lesson, as it was you who really gave me a lesson on giving, in the form of your receiving.

Chris later told me that he is not used to talking to a man so directly. This told me he knew exactly what I was asking when I asked the questions, and he answered them just the way I was to hear them. It was as though in a way I was serving him, as he is also a servant of God. This is true in many ways, and why we are to help others in their times of need. God does say in Galatians, chapter 5, verse 14, "For all the law is fulfilled in one word, even in this; Thou shalt love thy neighbor as thyself." So I was being a good neighbor by providing help to Chris as God himself would help him in the flesh. I was God's representative. Thank you, Lord, for my being able to serve you in this way.

We had worked up to lunch, and his wife had prepared a nice meal. I asked if I could bless the food before we ate. I had been taught by my brother-in-law, Michael, many years ago that it is an honor to go into someone's home to pray with them, to bless their home, thank God for all of their blessings, and to pray for help that they may need. He did not formally teach me or instruct me; it was just a matter of watching and observing his actions and then putting them into practice. This always made me feel really good inside, that they cared and loved me, when he and his wife, Maria, would pray for us.

I worked there about two more days and then came back to put in all the lights and outlets and to turn on the electricity to make everything work. I knew I was not going to ask for any payment—how could I accept money from someone who had thanked God all of his life and finally now asked for some help. As a servant of God, I was doing my job. Anyone with a heart would have done the same thing. I had given to someone in need of help through the gifts that God had gifted me with, and now I was returning his gift to one of his children.

He was absolutely taken aback when I said there would be no charge. He said, "What? My wife is not going to believe this." I told him that someday, someone will need help from him, and he should remember the day that he had received help. All along, while I was working with him, he did not know that there was not going to be any money involved. We had a good time laughing and praying together, along with just hard work. It was my time to give, or it was God's time to give to his child, using me as a vessel, because of his thanks in his prayers and his always glorifying God in his prayer by praising and thanking him.

One other lesson I learned is that, even though this was the lowest point in my life, with the construction of the house in the mountains, I could still give by helping others, even when I felt as though I should have been receiving help. This is really an awesome concept to remember and to use. Giving to others lightens our hearts of the burdens of everyday life.

Remember, it is a privilege to help someone in need. It is a privilege because this is God's way to share his fruit of the Spirit. "The fruit of the Spirit is love, joy, peace, longsuffering, gentleness, goodness, faith, meekness, temperance: against such there is no law. And they that are Christ's have crucified the flesh with the affections and lusts" (Galatians 5:22–24). So when you are asked to help someone, do it with a big, loving smile and with joy. You are extending God's love through you at this time. So be a good representative for God. Give all you can, for the window of opportunity to help someone is very small. If the time becomes longer than you had expected, then recognize how you can help that person to become closer to God through this window of opportunity.

Think about what I just said, and read it over again. Has someone asked you for help and you said no? It sure was easy to say no. It is very easy to say no to someone. God wants you to figure out a way to help others. Simply showing them a good direction to go, or sharing your knowledge, is of great benefit to them. God has given you gifts to help others. Yes, he has; all you have to do is to think of the things that you can do, and look at what you have. These are the gifts that God has blessed you with. Now it is time to share them with others.

Opportunities will come for you to use your gifts. Most of the time, an opportunity will not come at a convenient time. Yes, it is not when you want it to be. It will come when you are busy, very busy, or not ready in your heart. Recognize that you have to take the time, change the pace of what you are doing by slowing down, and then do the best that you can to give of your gifts. It is important to the people on the receiving end to receive when they need your gifted blessing from God. This is the opposite of being selfish and doing what you want, when you want to do it.

Are you guilty of doing what you want, when you want to, and how you want to do it? You know if you are. What can you do about it? You have actually done the very first thing, and that is to admit that you do this. As children of God, we know that we need the help of God to help correct this state of mind, so we ask God to correct this situation through his Son.

Let's pray:

> Dear God, in the name of your Son, Jesus, continually show me and open my eyes to correcting this way about me of having to control when things are to be done. Please give me the patience to accept things when they are to be done in *your* time. I recognize that you are in

control, and I serve you. Show me how I can serve you with all of your love. I give myself to you; speak to my heart when you want me to serve you. I thank you for all of the blessings that you have given to me as I'm honoring you, praising you, and sharing your goodness and love with others at my every opportunity. I pray these things in the name of your Son, Jesus. Amen.

Keep a Positive Attitude

One time, I was traveling by myself in my 1975 Mercury Bobcat, headed to Texas to go to school. It was during the summer of 1990, and I had left early in the morning. Going south on the interstate highway in Colorado, it was a beautiful morning, and I was just listening to the music on the radio when I saw a vehicle stopped along the side of the road. There were two young, Hispanic men standing by the car with a flat tire, the trunk open, and a spare tire leaning up against the car. I had just started into my journey and had only been on the road about two and a half hours. I knew I had to get where I was going, but I also knew that these two young men needed some help, and I was there and available. It was kind of inconvenient (but not really), so I could not find a good reason not to help them.

Remember, I was not as close to God at this time, but I did know when I could be of service to someone. Knowing what I know now I should find reasons to help someone, and I did do this on this occasion. I was to find reasons to help these guys in need of help. I could have just gone on down the road. The window of opportunity was then. If I had waited to do it on the way back seven days later, or on my day off, the window of opportunity to help them would not have been there at that time on the highway. You get my point. It did not hurt for me to stop, and come to find out, all they needed was a way to remove the tire and hold up the car with a jack stand. They had a full size car, like an older model Chevy Impala, that needed an old-style jack, and I did not have one of those.

I am not the kind of person to start something and not finish it, unless I have exhausted my every avenue to fix the problem. We looked around for something to put on the ground to raise my little scissor jack. They did not understand English, and I used hand signals to explain what I needed. We finally ended up using my spare tire on the ground and the scissor jack on top of it to lift the car up. It worked. I helped them with the change of the tire, and we went our separate ways.

I was really challenged to help someone then, and I did not give up on helping them until I had done everything I could. It was a little bit of a learning experience for me to continue until the problem was fixed, though. During this time in my life, everything had to be done with the exact right tool, or it simply could not get fixed. I was not open to different ideas of doing things, except doing them the right way. It had to be the right or correct way, or I waited to find the right tool from someone else. I was learning to be flexible. I felt good that I did not give up just because it was not convenient and because the exact, right tools were not there. I made it happen, and it was safe doing what we were doing.

Someday you may experience the same challenge. What will you do? I know you will find ways to make it happen by keeping a positive attitude.

Persevering in Helpfulness

Just recently I learned that when people need help, they may not ask for it. If they are asked if they need help, people will say no, but they do really, really need help. Remember this when you ask someone if you can help, by saying, "How can I help you?" Keep asking the person with sincerity, by saying, "Oh really, I want to help you, what can I do? There must be something I can do." If the person does not come up with anything, say, "Well, think on it for a little while, and I will call you to see what you need." The objective of the conversation is to succeed by helping and by finding out what you can do to help that person. It may take some time to get out of a person what you can do, but you will find a way to help. This is being a good Christian brother or sister.

Pride gets in the way of people's receiving help, many times. Do you know someone that has a lot of pride and will not ask for help? This is the person that you can practice working with. Find a way to show this person love by giving him or her something that he or she needs. If you think a person has everything, then pray for that person to receive God's love by his opening up his or her heart and mind. Everyone likes to be prayed for, so pray for something that you think the person needs. Simple, huh? Be a good neighbor by loving others in prayer. I believe people are placed into our lives because we are to help them and to pray for them. We are to ask God to open our hearts and minds to know how we are to help them and how we are to pray for what they need to make them better servants of God. Let's pray:

> Dear Father God, in the name of your Son, Jesus, please open up my heart and my mind to your ways, specifically to how I may help others with the gifts you have given to me. Show me in my mind when people need help, and give me the opportunity to help them with the gifts that you have given to me. Thank you so very much for being such a loving God and God of my life. Help me to recognize people in need of my gifts in the timing that is yours. Amen.

Everyone has a gift to give to others. What you have been taught to do is your gift to give to others. Channel this gift to do good for other people. Ask yourself, and ask God to help you, to focus on how you can make your gift available to other people, to help them to be better servants of God.

Overcoming Fear

One of the biggest challenges to overcome for Christians is fear. We overcome fear by trusting in God through his Son, Jesus. Christians overcome the challenge of fear by volunteering to do God's work. Part of God's work is to help your neighbor. Help your neighbor in whatever he or she needs help with, in your best judgment. Remember that God places people in your life so that you can pray for them, help them, and build them up to grow in the word of God that is in the Bible. Help them grow by setting a good example as you grow. When you see, sense, or feel fear, immediately bind it and tell it to leave you in the name of Jesus. Also ask that your fear be replaced with God's boldness. Whenever any evil spirit is removed, pray that an angelic spirit will take it's place.

Applying God's Word

Another of today's challenges is applying the Bible to today's experiences. The spiritual world is still the same today when the Bible was written, but the circumstances in which we live are different. That is why it is important to read books such as this one, to understand how God is working and is ever so present in today's living. He is very real and is very much a living God. His miracles are happening all around us. Once a person develops a sense of recognizing miracles, he or she can then notice how miracles do happen.

Identify Your Challenges

One important way God wants to bring you closer to him is through perseverance when things are not going your way. Identify for yourself exactly where the challenge is. What exactly is causing a problem? This is very important, to be able to identify the real problem. Whatever the problem is, check yourself to see if you have been giving in that area. Say, for instance, that a person steals from others—their employer, family members, or friends—then in God's eyes, by spiritual law, that person will be stolen from. Remember, what a person does (plants) is what he should expect to receive (harvest). If a person is critical to others, then that person should expect others to be critical in return. This goes on and on, with whatever behavior a person gives to another being received in return. If a person gives respect, then respect will be given in return. Always set the example for the behavior that you would like to see out of another person.

Here is a biblical example to model your behavior after: Luke 6:27–28 says, "But I say unto you which hear, Love your enemies, do good to them which hate you, Bless them that curse you, and pray for them which despitefully use you."

Here is a very good verse for what we were talking about, in Luke 6:37–38, "Judge not, and ye shall not be judged: condemn not, and ye shall not be condemned: forgive, and ye shall be forgiven: Give, and it shall be given unto you; good measure, pressed down, and shaken together, and running over, shall men give into your bosom. For with the same measure that ye mete withal it shall be measured to you again."

Wow, what powerful verses! Read these verses again and see the power that is in them. Give, and your receiving will be truly blessed, according to God's word of good measure unto you. The secret is the giving first, before the receiving. Selfishness gets in the way of this, as many people expect to always receive first and then give. God does not work this way. A person has to give first, as the Bible says.

When I think of this, I think of giving food to others; I can expect not to go hungry when I give lovingly to God's children, to feed them. When I give money to the church for God's work, I can expect not to want for money, as God will always provide for what I need. Galatians 6:7 reminds us, "Be not deceived; God is not mocked: for whatsoever a man soweth, that shall he also reap."

This is a law of how God works. Think about this and how you personally will apply this law. Every person is different in how he or she personally applies this in how he or she can give to others. Think about how you can personally give to others, in essence serving God, as you are now a servant of God. Yes, say this to yourself out loud: "I am a servant of God. I serve you, heavenly Father. Through your Son, Jesus, I come to you, as I have turned my life over to you, to learn and to abide in your loving ways. Thank you for this gift. Amen."

Remember, when we are being challenged, most of the time we should not expect an immediate response. The challenge has taken a while to get there as it was built upon, so it will take time to rebuild and to get around the challenge. To be Christ-like, acting and feeling with all of God's love, is the ultimate goal.

For a long time I did not understand why I had gotten goose bumps up and down the back of my legs, back, and neck during prayer, or while talking to a person or even a group of people. I thought it was the Holy Spirit. It *was* the Holy Spirit, in the sense that I was sensing the love of God, which would cause the goose bumps. The more powerful the sense and presence of love, the more powerful the goose bump experience. This is really awesome, as you may have experienced the same thing.

If you give something to someone and expect nothing in return, do not even accept credit for what you have given. Give God the credit when thanked. Let the person or people know that God provided through you, as you are a servant of God, and you are serving God by giving.

The Importance of Repentance

One substantially important way to get closer to God is through forsaking your sin for God's way of doing things. This is called repentance. The devil does not like this at all, so when you are changing your ways, just do it the way God wants you do it, or the devil will have time in the future to set out little traps for you, to keep your mind off of changing your ways. This is called distraction, as the devil wants to keep you from doing something good and loving, which is God's way.

I used to have a different excuse for not going to church every Sunday. I thought the excuses were mine, but it was really the devil telling me I was too busy to go to church. This was his distraction. I am sure you agree with this. So now that you agree, start going to church, and receive the Word of God, which is his food for us to live on.

By changing your ways to God's ways, and by asking God for help to change, you grow in your walk, with God being your best friend. This is so very important, because as you change, you are giving up ground that had previously belonged to the devil. He does not like that and will set out little traps of deceit. Do not fall for the traps, and conquer the devil by doing God's work. As you work and serve God, you will learn to recognize these little traps. Pray for help, and ask others to pray for you. Prayer teams at churches are available, as well as internet prayer groups.

The Discipline of Fasting

Sometimes God may want you to pray and fast to conquer difficult bondages or addictions of the world. A biblical passage that comes to mind is Matthew 17:18–21:

> And Jesus rebuked the devil; and he departed out of him: and the child was cured from that very hour. Then came the disciples to Jesus apart, and said, Why could not we cast him out? And Jesus said unto them, Because of your unbelief: for verily I say unto you, If ye have faith as a grain of mustard seed, ye shall say unto this mountain, Remove hence to yonder place; and it shall remove; and nothing shall be impossible unto you. Howbeit this kind goeth not out but by prayer and fasting.

God will reveal to you, once you ask him, what needs to be prayed for through the fasting process. Fasting is a very important process in getting closer to God, and there are many books out there that go into this a lot further than is mentioned here. It may be possible to fast and pray for others. This is an ultimate act of love for someone. The scripture above does not say that a person has to fast and pray for him or herself to remove selfish evil works of an addiction, bondage, evil spirit, or unchristian behavior.

Through one of my fasts, God revealed to me that I was selfish. I could not agree more, and I started looking more closely at myself and how I was being selfish. By God telling me this, it came from the Father Almighty himself. If someone else were to tell me this, I could easily say he or she did not know what he or she was talking about, and accuse that person of jealousy or something like that.

Next time you are tempted into a bondage or addiction, and you are about to do it, change and do something spiritual by buying a spiritual book at the book store or doing a good deed for someone instead. By doing this, you will no doubt find that you will get closer to God. Your reward is great by doing this, and joy will come upon you as you change and God sees you changing.

God bless you in your walk. God wants you to be closer to him, and you want to get closer to him also. You two will become the best of friends while you build upon your relationship of love throughout your lifetime. Pray to God that you want to be closer to him, and ask him to show you how. Between you and God, this is powerful friendship building at its finest. God loves you so very much, dear reader, my brother or sister in Christ.

Chapter Five

MY PERSONAL EXPERIENCES WITH GOD

I HAVE HAD SEVERAL significant experiences with God and look forward to his love, friendship, and companionship on a daily basis. One of the main reasons I'm sharing some of my experiences with you is to show you, by my personal testimony, of his existence, and how he is touching my life. You can experience his love, truth, and presence in your daily life also. It is just a matter of asking him to be present with you—a simple invitation into your heart or spirit.

God Protects Me

On June 1, 2007 (just a week ago from this writing), I was going home from work during a very rainy thunderstorm here in Colorado. It had been raining steadily for about 2 hours. I was driving my small, quarter-ton pickup truck (acquired from my dad about a year ago). The roads were very wet, and it was about 3 o'clock in the afternoon.

I was going the speed limit and had just started to turn a little to the right to go onto an expressway when the truck started to fishtail, and I lost control of the truck. I was hydroplaning (gliding on top of the water, with no contact or friction on the pavement). I could see large trees to my left that were getting closer as the truck slid in that direction. The truck did not offer much protection from hitting large trees. My eyes got big, and fear instantly overcame me. This occurred in probably a split second—it happened so very fast.

The back of the truck was sliding from side to side. Then I said out loud, "Father, please help me." At that very second, I felt a calm feeling overcome me. Then the truck corrected itself, and I continued down the road as if nothing had happened. Years ago I would have been very shaken up when something like this happened, but today was different. I felt the presence of God with the calm feeling, and I just knew he was (and is) taking care of me. I am just that confident. The devil had attacked me with a thought of fear, but I counterattacked by asking God the Father to help me. With a tear of love in my eye, I know he did help me and is always with us. Thank you, Lord God, for your continuous presence.

Thinking back, there are many things that could have happened. I could have hit the grass along the shoulder and started rolling sideways; I could have spun out of control and hit the trees or another vehicle; I could have been seriously injured or even killed. I am glad that no other vehicles were around me. It could only have been God there protecting me.

What an awesome God, indeed! I know this to be fact. He sure wants you to receive this book into your hands, to bless you with his information and through the example of my testimony, giving all credit, honor, and praise to God the Father Almighty for his grace, presence, and love.

Believe this with all of your heart, mind, and God's love in the manner which this book is intended, without any distortion of the devil.

God Has a Sense of Humor

It was a cold, wintry night in January of the year 2003, about 5:30 P.M. There had been a short-blowing blizzard that day, making it a typical cold day. There was a regularly scheduled, monthly elder's meeting at church, and as I was the chairman of the board, I had prepared an agenda for the elders, as I usually do. We were in a special meeting room within the church that is decorated and has a lot of church history in it. The table at which all the elders were seated on this particular evening was rather long, and there were about ten elders present. I had passed around and distributed monthly business papers, along with the written agenda. It was a few minutes after starting time, and I had decided to go ahead and start. It is customary to pray for the meeting before we start, and I always ask if there is someone who would like to open the meeting in prayer. This allows the Holy Spirit freedom to work within each and every elder to present a prayer that is on the heart of the elder.

It had been some time since I had prayed an opening prayer, and I had offered to see if anyone would like to open in prayer. There was no response, and I knew it was meant for me to open the meeting in prayer. I had even sensed a slowing in time with a presence of the Holy Spirit. So I opened the meeting with an invitation for God to be with us and guide us in our meeting.

Throughout the meeting, we conducted our usual business, and about an hour later, I had closed the meeting with prayer, also with the conclusion of the Lord's Prayer by all present. Upon conclusion of the prayer, I had a very pressing need to go to the restroom. So I excused myself rather hurriedly and returned within just about one minute. When I returned, no one was there. Usually elders stand around for a few minutes to discuss different items and then leave. I found this to be very unusual and began to look around in the kitchen and then down the hallway. No one was there. I just could not believe it. So I looked again. I looked outside through the window of the hallway, and down the hallway in the direction of the sanctuary. I could find no one anywhere. I thought to myself, *Well, I guess I will go.* So I gathered up my paperwork and proceeded out the door of the meeting room. I had to turn off the lights before going out of the room, so I used my left hand and pushed the three switches in the downward direction to turn them off. Once I did this and the lights were off, I heard this very loud, echoing voice within the room. The voice said, "Good night."

I immediately turned the lights back on, amazed by the voice. I again walked and looked around the room, hallway, and kitchen. No one was there. I turned the lights off once again and began thinking about how something like this could happen. The only reasonable thought I could come up with is that God has a sense of humor. During my prayers, I had invited God to be present in the beginning of the meeting and had honored him and praised him with the closing prayer, with unity and agreement of the elders at the meeting. This was a powerful and most amazing experience. So he had spoken to me, just to say that, yes, there is someone here in God's house, as I was so intently looking for someone. So he humorously acknowledged his presence by saying goodnight.

Remember that there are two Bible verses that talk about church meetings, and it is these two verses that make church meetings strong. They are in the book of Matthew, chapter

18, verses 19 and 20, "Again I say unto you, That if two of you agree on earth as touching any thing that they shall ask, it shall be done for them of my Father which is in heaven. For where two or three are gathered together in My name, there am I in the midst of them."

The power of these two verses is the reason I believe I heard God saying goodnight to me in his own way, to let me know that, yes, there is someone here, not just an empty room. His Spirit is in his house at all times. During the next month's elder's meeting, I shared this with the group, as I felt it only appropriate to do so. Thank you, Lord, for your invisible presence and the comfort of knowing that you are always here with us. Amen.

Horse Rescue

During the summer of 1993, I wanted to go hiking on the north side of Pike's Peak Mountain. It was a beautiful, warm, dry, summer day in Colorado. I owned a truck with a small camper shell on it, and I headed out. In no time at all, I was traveling on a dirt road along the Rampart Range. There were not many people traveling on the road, as it was a weekday.

While I drove along, I saw a pickup truck ahead, with a horse trailer behind it, parked in the opposite direction that I was traveling. I slowed down and recognized one of the two men who were at the back of the trailer doing something. I drove past, but I sensed that something was wrong. I was not even sure if there were horses in the trailer until I turned around, got out, and walked over to see the guys. There was one horse on the left side of a two-stall horse trailer.

I know almost nothing about horses, except that they have four legs and hooves. One of the men, the one I knew, had a hold on the bridle that goes into the horse's mouth and around the head (calming the horse). The horse had somehow placed its right rear leg over the divider between the two stalls. All I remember hearing was the man saying how the horse was going to get gutted and split open through its belly, implying that the horse was going to unknowingly kill itself. The divider was tall; the only way the horse could have gotten that way was by kicking.

I had to change the attitude in the atmosphere, because it was too negative. I had to be positive and change the course of action to an absolutely positive scenario. So I started thinking about what might work. The only thing that was going to work was taking the divider apart so the horse could walk out of the trailer.

I told the men that the divider needed to be taken apart, and all I got was, "Oh no, the horse is going to get gutted." I responded with a firm, "No, it's not. Let's take apart the divider." So we proceeded to take it apart by lowering the divider, and the horse walked out without any harm. What a relief (whew)! I shook the men's hands and proceeded on with my hiking adventure.

This story is short, but it shows how to have a positive influence to change situations that could turn out badly because of speaking bad thoughts. Speak about things in the way you want them to be. Remember, our spoken words have the power of life and death. Proverbs 18:21 says, "Death and life are in the power of the tongue: and they that love it shall eat the fruit thereof."

In this case, the words that I spoke changed the expected death of the horse to life. I was really bothered about how negative this person was, and now I understand that it was fear that caused the negativity.

So what can I do today for this person? I can pray for the person, that fear will be bound in the name and shed blood of Jesus. We are to pray for one another, as stated in the book of James, chapter 5, verse 16: "Confess your faults one to another, and pray one for another, that ye may be healed. The effectual fervent prayer of a righteous man availeth much."

I now know that this was a divine appointment for me to be there to help. I did what was natural for me to do. Thank you, Lord, for allowing me to serve you in this way. Amen.

The men probably do not know all the spiritual events that happened. But I know that it is spiritual, and people help me every day. We need other people. We are to apply biblical passages into our lives and understand them. These are principles of life that we are to live. We are to understand that this is how God works in our every day lives.

God's Miracle Saves Two Boy Scouts

I am a Boy Scout leader in the troop sponsored and chartered by our church. (There are many girl and boy scouting organizations that are sponsored by churches.) As a troop, we make an effort to go camping at least once a month. In the latter part of February, 2003, we had scheduled to go on a winter campout along the front range of the Rocky Mountains on an Army Post. This is always a treat, because this gives the scouts an opportunity to eat some food prepared by army cooks in a military dining facility and environment.

It snows several times during the year along the front range of the mountains; however, it does not stay for very long. The sun melts it within a few days. We had planned to sleep in tents for Friday and Saturday night. We would eat a light breakfast and lunch on Saturday, go swimming in a heated, indoor pool at the Army Post, eat at the dining facility, go bowling, and then return to the camp and go to sleep for the night. We would then get up in the morning, eat breakfast, and then head for home. It is always a fast weekend, with lots of fun.

When my father was in the army, we were stationed at this post in Colorado Springs. While I was a Boy Scout, I had the privilege of doing all these things, and had even camped at this campsite. There is always plenty of firewood, because we are in the trees, in a mountain setting. There are even some flagpoles on the site to conduct flag ceremonies.

We arrived at the campsite around 6:30 P.M., and of course, it was already dark. The ground was cold and frozen, and the air was about 30 degrees, but it was dry, and there was no snow on the ground. We set up our three tents, with 2 scouts in one tent, three in another, and the two adults in another. All the scouts were about 14 years old. We started a fire in one of the fire pits, and we all sat around chatting. Someone had brought some of those good ol' giant marshmallows, so we roasted some of those on sticks, and boy, those sure tasted good over an open campfire. We told some stories and jokes, and about 10 P.M., we put some water on the fire to put it out and headed for our tents and sleep.

On Saturday morning we got up, had some breakfast, and then went on a nature hike through the woods before returning for some lunch. We were scheduled to go swimming at 1 P.M. This always warms everyone up, and it is a lot of fun. After swimming, we all put on our Scout uniforms with our bright fluorescent orange neckerchiefs. Off we went, and while we were eating dinner, the boys had a chance to talk to some of the soldiers.

I have always enjoyed eating in the dining facilities, known to me in my younger years as "mess halls." My father is a retired Army mess sergeant, which means he was a cook while he was serving our country during the thirty years that he was in. I remember going to mess halls on Thanksgiving and Christmas to eat the holiday meals there. It was always a joyous feast.

I was a paperboy, delivering papers on Post during my 5th through 8th grade years. On the weekends I would go through the barracks wearing the old front and back cloth paper bags to sell newspapers to the soldiers to earn extra money. The paper bag would have the name of the newspaper on the front and back. I was proud to carry this on my shoulders, as I had a job. For youngsters my age it was hard to find steady work on an Army Post. It was during this time that I would walk through the mess halls and ask for a glass of chocolate milk. This was a treat, and it will always be a good memory of my childhood.

Anyway, back to the weekend campout. After we finished eating at the dining facility, we headed over to the bowling alley. At this time it had started to snow, and it was a wet snow with large snow flakes. We played a couple of games, then left to go back to the camp, which was about 5 miles away.

It was still snowing when we got to camp. We expected it to stop snowing at any time. We did not want to get wet, so we all went on into our tents to go to sleep. Through the night, we would knock the snow off the tent. At about 2 o'clock in the morning I woke up, having the unprecedented urge to see if I could see the two tents outside. I was in my sleeping bag, which had a sleeping pad underneath it to insulate me from the ground. I opened up the tent to look outside. It was still snowing those big snow flakes. I remember asking the other adult leader, as he was half awake, "Where is the other tent?" I could see one of the two tents, but not the other.

I kept trying to look through the falling snow flakes to see the other tent. I just could not see the other tent. I had to be able to see the other tent. It was just not there to see. This was strange and dreamlike. I remember saying out loud three or more times, "Where is the other tent?" as I was trying to wake up. Early in the morning, and with my being half asleep, the tent that I could see seemed so far away.

I gave up on trying to see the tent, and I decided to go out into the storm to find it. I put on my shoes to go look for it. When I had gotten over to where I thought the tent should be, I saw that the tent had fallen in on the two boys from the weight of the snow. The tent had formed and molded around the bodies of the two boys. I used my foot to nudge the boys to get a response from them while I was brushing the snow off the tent to set it back up. There was no response; I thought that they were in a deep sleep.

While I was going around and around the tent, I was joyous with laughter that I had been there to put the tent up right for these two young Christians. I knew in faith and love that all was well. It just, I mean, it could not be any other way. I was full of confidence that all that was needed was to set up the tent. When I got the tent up, I flexed it several times to pump air into the tent; it was even as if God himself was pumping air into their lungs.

I instructed the boys in the tent to keep the snow off the tent by hitting the sides of the tent. No response. Keeping 100% positive and absolutely knowing that nothing was wrong, I instructed the boys to keep the snow off the tent. Then I went over to the other tent and instructed those boys to keep an eye on the other tent, to make sure snow was kept off of it. Meanwhile, it was still snowing large snowflakes.

I went on back to my tent. In the morning, everything was fine, as if it were just another morning. We all got up, broke camp, cleaned what we could of the area, and left to go home. There was about 6 inches of wet snow on

the ground. Thinking back, I realized the boys could have suffocated. This scared me, as it never even had entered my mind at the time. I was 100% positive in my mind, spirit, and in my speaking. I will not know on this earth, if the boys had suffocated, if CPR would or would not have revived them.

There have been other times when I have been with other people when I have had to be extremely positive, like I was with the re-erecting of the tent. I have to speak positively and sometimes renounce the negative thoughts. Not one negative thought had gone through my mind while setting up the tent, only that it just needed to be put back up. My faith, positive thinking, joyous intervention, love for the boys, and God's supreme and almighty love for them saved these two boys. All of this together created a miracle from God.

This brings tears to my eyes about how awesome God is and all of his love. I did not realize all the steps of this miracle until this writing. I know my touching them physically had a spiritual effect, along with my speaking in joy and confidence. I want to give all the credit to God, but I cannot help but to think and know that I had a lot to do with this miracle. God wants all of us to live by great faith, positive thinking, God's joy in knowing positive outcomes, prayer, love, and knowing God's supreme, almighty love. The mixture for all of this is a miracle in our grasp to perform, should everything be in alignment.

At the time I felt that the only mission I had to do was to set up the tent, and God would do the rest. This happens when you are a servant of God. You do what is expected, and he does the rest. You are his tool to do what he wants, when he wants. When I see the two boys today, I look at them in amazement, and I wonder what God has planned for them in the future, because they certainly are special.

These boys are blessed and have my total respect of God protecting them. It puts a lump in my throat, knowing the power of God and how he truly does communicate with us. We just have to listen and act on it. God knew the exact words to motivate me to wake up, get my attention in his own personal way, and take care of this situation. Thank you, Lord God, for taking care of us while we go camping and on scouting activities.

We make it a practice to put in a prayer request to our church congregation for our protection when we go out. This is an example of God's people's prayers at work. Many times we have to physically intervene and do what we are best at, and do the right thing at that time. It is best to do the right thing no matter what the consequence is. This way we know in our hearts that we did do the right thing, and this we can live with. Later, through God's wisdom, we may choose to do something different, as we are in a different time in our life, with different circumstances.

Our Loving God Shows Me His Power in New Mexico

Several years ago I had decided to buy a vehicle out of state. I wanted to take a look at it, but it was in Phoenix, Arizona. So I purchased an airline ticket and flew to Arizona. I arranged to meet the gentleman, and he picked me up at the airport. I liked the car, so I purchased it, and now all I had to do was drive it home. I did not want to stay the night anywhere, so I just pulled over in the back of a motel parking lot, let the rear seat down, and used my jacket for a blanket. It was a long, cold night somewhere in southern New Mexico, and I was cold. The month was March or April.

About 5 o'clock in the morning, I decided to start the car to warm up, then I decided to start traveling again. I really like the early morning, as everything wakes up and seems so fresh, new, and vibrant. A couple hours later, the sun was warming up the day, shining brightly, with no clouds in the sky. It was just a beautiful morning.

The main interstate running north-south is I-25, and it was about 8 o'clock in the morning on a Friday. There was not as much traffic as I had thought there would be going through the town of Albuquerque. I do not remember seeing cars behind me, in front of me, or on the other side of the divided highway. All I remember seeing was a man walking along the right shoulder of the road. He was not carrying anything in his hands, but he appeared to be going somewhere.

I do not make a habit of picking anyone up along the side of the road. Today I did not plan on it either. I was traveling at a speed of about 55 miles per hour, in the right lane. I passed the man, and the next thing I knew, it felt as though someone else had taken control of the steering wheel, and I pulled over as if to give the man a ride. I had to slow down, of course, so I was about 80–100 yards in front of the man on the right shoulder. I don't know what happened, it happened so quickly. All I know is that something came over me or the steering wheel—I don't know which—and here I was, waiting for the man to come up to the side of the car. I unlocked the car door, and he came up and opened the door. I asked him if he would like a ride, and he said yes and got in.

I was nervous, and we talked a little. He said that his nephew told him he had to go to the doctor today to get his kidney dialysis. I told him I was a little nervous, and he said he was too. He was in his mid-fifties to early sixties. He mentioned that he prayed to God for protection for the trip to the doctor today, as he had no transportation. I think he was just a little nervous about going to see the doctor in general. I had mentioned something about being a Christian, and when we had a conversation about God, we both felt comfortable with each other.

I kept the conversation going by asking him where he needed to go to get his medical treatment. He said I could drop him off at an exit, and he could go from there. I did not think this was the best thing to do, as I had plenty of time, was not in a real hurry, and did not have any emergencies going on. So I drove him right to the doctor's office. Dropping him off in the parking lot, I made sure he entered the building, and then I went on my way back to Colorado.

I think God had planned everything for me to be at the right place at the right time, even arranging no cars to be in the vicinity of the meeting to distract me or to keep me from picking him up and giving him a ride. Two prayers had taken place before the meeting: one for my safe travels and one for his safe travels. Prayers are being answered by God for all who are praying. I do not know the outcome of the gentlemen's doctor's visit, but I do feel as though it was needed to build my faith, the man's faith, and your faith in God's answering prayers. Many times the answer is not obvious, but there are other times that it is very obvious. Just watch, look, and listen. Thank you, Lord, for the opportunity to be your servant.

Chapter Six

WHAT GOD WANTS YOU TO KNOW ABOUT ANGER

GOD WANTS TO make you aware that he is very concerned about the amount of anger in the world. My purpose in making you, the reader, aware of this is to bring the truth to light—in other words, to weaken the nature of anger itself.

The first and most important thing to know when praying for someone who has anger is to pray for God's protection for yourself, so the angry spirit does not come onto you or go anywhere else when you bind it in the name and shed blood of Jesus. As a prayer warrior for God, you must know this. In Matthew 16:19 it states, "And I will give unto thee the keys of the kingdom of heaven: and whatsoever thou shalt bind on earth shall be bound in heaven: and whatsoever thou shalt loose on earth shall be loosed in heaven."

So be careful what you speak, how you say it, and what you are bringing upon yourself and people around you. Speak life and encouragement unto others at all times.

I would like to explain to you what happens with anger from a spiritual aspect, how it comes about, how it stays with a person by manifestation, and how it can be subdued, bound, or simply gotten rid of.

Anger comes about when people feel as though they are unloved, and how they deal with anger within themselves will affect how they interact with people around them. Anger also comes about within people when they feel as though they are being pushed around, and they cannot do anything about it at that time. They will take this anger out in a different way. Interesting concepts, yes? I am speaking generally now and will get more specific by using examples.

To me anger is one of many evil emotions of the world that with prayer can be prayed away. In Ephesians 4:26–27 it states, "Be ye angry, and sin not: let not the sun go down upon your wrath: Neither give place to the devil." A person must not allow this emotion to manifest itself within ones mind as it can grow and sometimes a person will take actions that they normally would not. In Romans 12:21 it states, "Be not overcome of evil, but overcome evil with good." Low self-esteem may accompany the angry spirit, along with the evil spirits of fear and selfishness. This is not a good combination, and it can result in some very bad things happening. Once the main evil spirit is bound in the name of Jesus, the other evil spirits will leave.

Angry people do not know how to get rid of being angry, so they look for relief by doing what they think makes them feel better. Most of the time, this means making others feel as bad, or worse, than they are feeling. So they go around making other people's lives as miserable as theirs.

You have probably heard the saying, "Misery loves company." Well, to an unchurched person this may be so; however, with a churched person, this can be corrected by knowing how to recognize it, pray against it, pray for protection of yourself and others, and pray for love to come into your life as well as the lives of others. The problem with the statement, "Misery loves company," is that when people are miserable and want others to be miserable with them, that's when God shows them through conviction that they are wrong. Then they have to live with guilt.

How will this guilt leave? Things will be corrected only by forgiving others, by asking the victims for forgiveness, and by asking God to forgive them for what they have done. Then the person must make sure that the bad example he or she has set will not be passed onto his or her offspring. Otherwise the potential for children to follow in their parents' footsteps is very likely. Once people are aware, they now have the power to stop the current and future situation of this behavior. If the behavior gets really bad, God may at some time allow them to be corrected. Remember that Satan is lurking at all times, seeking to destroy us. When we become aware of his presence in a certain behavior, we simply state, "In the name of Jesus, I renounce this behavior and do not accept it. Leave now and forever. God, please help me to replace this behavior with a loving nature. Amen."

Do you see people walking around destroying material items? This is a form of anger. If this person is a child, he or she is counting on his or her parents to help and to understand how he or she feels. If the parents or someone else does not intervene, then the anger grows into bigger forms of destruction. Okay, you are beginning to see what I am saying can be applied to the people around you. What can you do about it? First of all, people just need to know that they are loved. They need to know that they are loved by you, by people around them, and most importantly, by God the Almighty Father. Invite them to go to church with you, a Bible study, or a church event. Show them the abundant love that is within the church body.

People can help themselves with anger by forgiving others for what they have done to them, and by developing a closer relationship with their Father God, including the Father, the Son Jesus, and the Holy Ghost. God wants you and all his children closer to him. No matter what has been done to a person, that person must forgive the offender or offenders in order to be healed and release the feelings of hurt. This can only be done by asking God through his Son, Jesus, to help that person to forgive and release the hurt feelings. This is so very important to know. Go back and read the last sentence again and understand it.

So to summarize a little, people will benefit by recognizing anger within themselves and others, with the ultimate goal of getting rid of the angry feelings. Okay, how does an answer come about to help get rid of what is causing the angry feelings in the first place? God's Ten Commandments must be listened to and obeyed. Secondly, God's principles in the Bible, many mentioned throughout this book, must be applied, one of which is forgiveness.

Read verse 37 in the 6th chapter of Luke: "Judge not, and ye shall not be judged: condemn not, and ye shall not be condemned: forgive, and ye shall be forgiven." This verse says that what you give to others is what you get as a spiritual principle. What you do to others is what you are going to receive from others.

God wants you to know that a person has to ask him for the answer to his or her problem, and to get that answer, he or she has to start applying God's laws and principles. If people decide to do things on their own, society has a way of keeping them housed in jails and prisons. People learn that if they do not comply with society, then they are placed away from society. They may or may not understand why they are there. Not only are they in a physical prison, they are in a mental prison, without a way out except through

God. God is the only way for them to receive peace in their minds, their hearts, and their souls.

To receive God's fruit on earth is to receive love, joy, peace, longsuffering, gentleness, goodness, and faith, as stated in chapter 5 of Galatians, verse 22. Go to this verse, and other verses in the Bible that I quote, and read the verses around them to get a more meaningful and complete understanding of the verse.

God can prevail in their lives with a simple invitation from them for God to come into their lives and hearts. Then it is a matter of reading and studying the Bible, and practicing his commandments, principles, and ways in everyday life—every minute of every day.

There is a balance of good and bad, being mostly good to stay out of prison. To end up in prison, these people allowed Satan to control their minds and actions. They chose to be controlled by the dark side of this earth.

To choose life is to choose God and his ways and to pray to receive understanding and God's wisdom, as stated in the 4th chapter of Proverbs. The 7th chapter of Proverbs, verses 1 and 4 are also very good to understand. Pray for this understanding, and God will give you the understanding that you need at this time in your life. Keep asking for wisdom throughout your life, because you will need it as you grow in God's love and his ways.

Chapter Seven

WHY YOU SHOULD PERSEVERE

GOD WANTS YOU to become closer to him by persevering when you feel as though you should give up. When you're facing something that is very tough, this is when God wants you to trust in him and press on to do what is challenging you. Pray for your opposition and bless them. Matthew 5:44 says, "But I say unto you, Love your enemies, bless them that curse you, do good to them that hate you, and pray for them which despitefully use you, and persecute you."

Perseverance means that when you are being challenged, that is the time to give lovingly. This is also a time to pray for this wonderful ability. Let's pray on our knees this time; smile, knowing in faith and love for God that your prayer is already answered:

> Father God, I praise you and honor you by humbling myself to you through your Son, Jesus. I know I can only get to you through your Son, Jesus. I thank you for the ability and strength to persevere daily in your will

and your way, with all the love that you have for me. Allow me to set the example of perseverance because of your strengthening me. Lift me up so I may honor you. Amen.

When people are challenged, they want to withdraw, and they expect others to give to them because they are in trouble. Instead, this is the time to give to others and let the blessings come from God. This is an act of unselfishness. People may think they have nothing to give; however, they still have more than others in the world.

Material items only have a value to those who value them. Some people keep items of value because it seems to give them worth. I used to keep every item of value, storing them somewhere in our house—usually in a box, or stored on a shelf somewhere—but always in a safe place. These things gave me a sense of worth and value. I would keep things that people had given to me so that I could remember the love they had given to me. I still do, but I do not put the item above God's love for me.

I still value items that someone has given to me, as it represents their love for me. If the item wears out or gets damaged, I know the item served a purpose, and I thank God for the gift that the person has given to me, and I keep their love for me in that special place in my heart.

I know that God loves you and me so very much, and he will do anything in his power to get you and everyone else. This is why he needs your prayer for others.

When challenges come upon you, ask for prayer from others. Keep on praying for protection, and find out if the challenge comes from a selfish way, mirroring something that you have done in the past. Remember Galatians 6:7, "Be not deceived; God is not mocked: for whatsoever a man soweth, that shall he also reap." In other words, if people steal, they should expect to be stolen from. If they help others, then they can expect others to help them. If a person only helps others here and there, then they should only expect to be helped here and there.

For a long time I thought the challenges that I have faced were actually from a person. This is not true. I had done something to others in the past, but not as big a challenge as was given to me. So when I did receive the challenge, it was of greater magnitude, of course. I think this is God's way of getting our attention, so we'll stop doing what we've done to others in the past.

For instance, I started paying taxes for other people's property several years ago, with the intention of acquiring their property to make myself more valuable and to make more money. This I did by going to tax lien sales held by the county I live in and in surrounding counties. I convinced myself that I had to; I had to learn to be businesslike, without emotion. I know now that this is wrong. Ultimately, the person would have to pay me a fair amount of interest money, or in time they would lose their property. Of course, I would pay their taxes from year to year.

Many people do not know that they can lose their house or property if they choose not to pay the taxes. The county in which they live does not care who pays the taxes, just as long as the taxes are paid. So why not pay someone else's taxes—if they want to keep the property, then they can pay you the interest that is due to you, or you (as the tax lien holder) can legally take over the property and continue paying the yearly taxes too. It is a long process, and it takes several years to actually acquire a property.

Well, I did acquire a property, and while I was going through the legal process, the owner of the property asked me through my lawyer if I would return the property with them paying me the interest money only. I knew the property was worth several thousand dollars, versus maybe a thousand dollars of repayment of interest, and legally I would get the property anyway. Most of the time people are blinded by the law and do not really think that they will lose the property, and it is sad that they really do. People think, "This cannot happen, and it's not really happening; God will not allow this." Many people lose properties all the time by being ignorant.

I thought that what is legal is right. Oh, how wrong I was! Please do not be deceived by this trap to make money, as I was. God had more to say about this, and I am glad that I learned from my mistake. Even though it was legal, it was not right in God's eyes. The person I took the property from worked and probably tithed to God with the earnings of his or her work to pay for the property. I do not know, but I do know that the same thing happened to me. Money, along with property, was taken from me in the same way that I had taken property from the owner, except I lost ten times the amount, and more. Not only did I lose money and labor hours, I lost equity—money that was invested into the house and property, which was my profit to repay the money I used out of my pocket to finish building the house. Money was stolen from me, and I lost a lot of money, as I could not sell the house to get the profit out. The lender that we borrowed money from made lots of money in interest from us on money that was actually stolen from us.

Listen to this statement again: I was paying interest on money that was stolen from us. So there were two different things that I had done to someone else in the past which were now happening to me, and both at the same time. One was that the very same thing I had done in acquiring a property earlier was being done to me. And the other happened several years ago, when we acquired a car that a lender had repossessed from someone, and that person had to pay on the loan the difference that we did not pay. So he or she was paying on a car which we were driving and that he or she did not have.

This is the same thing that we are doing. We are currently paying on a loan for construction materials that were put into a house that we now do not own. This amount is over ten times the amount that we had acquired from the car. The lesson I have learned is that even though a human process may be legal in business, it may not be the right thing to do by God's standard. So be careful how you earn a living.

In the spiritual realm, the evil spirits of sin surround us and I have seen that they can actually be revealed by people with discernment. I personally have been given this gift and God has given me a word of revelation on occasion. This is awesome in itself. The words of caution are that sin within a person many times attracts other people of the same sin such as theft or stealing. I believe if a person steals then that person will be stolen from at one time or another but with a greater degree than the original sin of theft. To do this Satan brings in his reinforcements to destroy you and break you. He sets up a trap that you think is safe, like a predator. He stalks you for an opening of sin or greed in your life, and then he slowly attacks. He is always out, seeking you, tempting you to slip up and listen to his stupidity. In 1 Peter 5:8 it says, "Be sober, be vigilant; because your adversary the devil, as a roaring lion, walketh about, seeking whom he may devour."

This is why we persevere. Pray—pray for others, and ask for prayer. We have to insist that Satan leave us alone, always in the name of Jesus. We have to pray more. He wants to make us stumble so we keep from praying. So no matter what the challenge, we keep praying, and pray even harder. You are now a prayer warrior for God.

Keep in mind that nothing is free. We always seem to pay a price if we take advantage of someone. If it does not seem right to you, but it is legal, watch out. As you can see, dear reader, I learned this the hard way. My eyes were opened to see that what I had done in the past was not right, and an opportunity came for the devil to do to me what I had done to others, but in a bigger way, in order to make me stumble and to challenge me. So I persevered, learned my lessons, asked God for forgiveness for what I had done wrong, and now I am a better person for it.

As you can see, the main idea to understand and learn from is to figure out why a challenge has come upon us in the first place. You can do this by asking God to show you. Then your answers will come to your mind, just like they did for me.

For a long time, I did not understand why these things happened, and I was blaming others, when in the spiritual realm I had caused everything to happen to me all on my own. So I can only blame myself for what has happened to me, and for what may even happen in the future. What I see now is that in a lot of jobs, people have an opportunity to take advantage of other good people who trust them. If they listen to the wrong voice, they too will sooner or later be snagged in a web of despair like I was. It was the most grueling experience that I have ever endured. So now it becomes my testimony, as I have overcome by the blood of the Lamb. Revelations 12:11 says, "And they overcame him by the blood of the Lamb, and by the word of their testimony; and they loved not their lives unto the death."

The bottom line here is to talk and act on what your heart says, not your mind. Your mind can be filled with the wrong thoughts from the dark of the devil. God lives in our hearts. Be a child of God; admit you are his and belong to God. Just speak this out loud. "I am a child of God, in the name and blood of Jesus. Amen."

Chapter Eight

GOD'S GIFTS FOR YOU

GOD WANTS YOU to draw closer to him by giving you his gifts, so you may use those gifts to serve other people while praising him. The ultimate gift that God has given to all people is the life and blood of his Son, Jesus. Jesus died for you on the cross many years ago so that you may have forgiveness of sins. What does this really mean? Well, it means that all you have to do is ask God in the name of his Son, Jesus, to forgive you of what you have done wrong. The prayer can go like this:

> Dear Heavenly Father, in the name and shed blood of your Son, Jesus, please forgive me for____________ (fill in the blank here with the things that you have done wrong). Please show me and give me the strength to overcome this behavior, as I know I cannot do this by myself. Thank you, Lord, for the love you have for me, and continue to bless me with your love. Amen.

Now God wants you to forgive all of the people who have ever done anything to you. Yes, that is what I said, you have to forgive them. While you are praying, God will show you in your mind the people you have to forgive. Speak out loud the name of the person who wronged you, and say out loud, "I forgive you, _________ (fill in the name of the person who is on your mind). That was easy, wasn't it? Make a list of people, and continue to forgive them, and pray that they will be blessed by God.

God's Gift of Prayer

I feel God puts people in our path now, in the future, and in the past, so that we may pray for them. We all need prayer, as prayer is the most powerful thing that we can do for a person. Pray to build a person up and encourage him or her. With a lot of feeling within your heart, a prayer can go like this:

> Dear Heavenly Father, in the name of your Son, Jesus, open my mind and heart to forgive _____________ , as I hereby release this person to you, and I no longer keep the bad feelings that I have for this person. I now only think of the good things this person has done for me. I love this person and want you to bless this person so that this person will now give love to others. Give this person the strength to come to you also, to overcome his/her weaknesses. Amen.

Whenever God brings this person to your mind, pray a prayer of blessing onto this person. Keep praying for all of the people that God puts into your mind. This is actually a gift, to be able to pray for others. As you pray for others, you are becoming like God by loving all people, specifically the ones whom God has placed into your life. When you love others, this allows the doors to be opened for others to love you.

One of the best prayers to pray is just the name of Jesus. Pray, "Jesus, Jesus, Jesus." Pray this several times, out loud, with love. Keep repeating this whenever you feel like loving God. Feel the love for God when saying the name of Jesus over and over. Whenever you feel as though you want company, just say his name out loud or whisper it softly. This is very powerful. Tell Jesus that you love him. "Jesus, I love you. Jesus, Jesus, I love you." Say this with feeling, from your heart, and really mean it. It really feels good, and by saying this daily, you will become closer to God.

"Ask, and it shall be given you; seek, and ye shall find; knock and it shall be opened unto you" (Matthew 7:7). One popular way of praying is prayer circles. I see them more and more. A prayer circle is when two or more people gather together in the name of Jesus, and all the people stand in a circle, holding hands. Each person bows his or her head. One person starts the prayer, then it proceeds to the next person, and the prayer completes its circle. This is very powerful unity. A good way to end the prayer is to recite the Lord's Prayer and then praise God with a cheerful song.

This is a good idea for families to use around the dinner (or breakfast) table, during gatherings, family reunions, in the evenings, or anytime people wish to pray together with their families, or with other like-minded people. If there is a specific item of interest to be prayed for, it is a good idea to talk about it first, before prayer starts, so everyone is in agreement. During the prayer, each person softly states his or her agreement, feels it in his or her heart, and extends his or her brotherly or sisterly love to the person being prayed for.

Praying for others in groups is very powerful. Prayers for others can take place over the phone or even the internet.

There are prayer groups on the internet that will pray for a person, and there is also the opportunity to pray for other people's requests. I personally pray for others regularly on the internet, and I also request prayer. This is really awesome. Pray on, brothers and sisters in Christ.

God's Gifts of Talents & Abilities

God blesses many people with gifts that benefit themselves as well as others. These gifts are everything that a person does that is acceptable to society. A gift may be simply being able to make a person laugh, or being able to sing a song. Think of all your gifts that God has given to you. Write them down on a list, and now, thank God for all of your gifts.

The secret here on earth is to keep these gifts, as they may be taken away from you. Ask God for his wisdom, to keep the gifts that he has given to you, and most importantly, thank God for all of the gifts that he has given to you.

God's Gift of Giving

One way to honor and praise God is to give (tithe) money that you have earned with your gifts to a church of your choosing. This is to be done with your first fruits, which means that you give ten percent from your earnings without taking money first to go buy something. Now you are learning the gift of giving. Today there are different views on the percentage to give, and I prefer to give ten percent.

The way of the world is to always want to be the receiver of gifts. People always say to themselves, "I am a good person, and they should give to me." Well, in God's world, the way he is (and the way he wants you closer to him) is to give to others even when you think you are not able. When you give, you then release the power of receiving. Re-read that last sentence; it is very important. When you give, you then release the power of receiving. This means, when you give, you release God's love within you to another person. Isn't that powerful? You are representing God by giving his love. By being kind to others and loving others, you are also representing him.

Remember that God is love. Look around you for a mentor who is a loving person, and sit down and talk with this person. Get ideas on how you can become a more loving person. After you talk to that person, act on how you may become a more loving person. Go out of your way to do something nice for a person. Practice saying good things about other people and giving—yes, I said giving—compliments to other people. Whatever you give, you will become abundant in that gift. Does this happen right away? Not always. It is always in God's time. When God is ready for you to receive, he will give it to you. One way this gift becomes abundant to you is that once it is released from being important to you, it is no longer bondage upon you or preventing you from being able to keep God first and number one in your life.

God's Gift of Encouragement

God wants you to become closer to him by learning a new language of speaking life and encouragement onto others. By giving others verbal encouragement, you are representing God by encouraging them. This is also a gift that God has given to you so that you may also be encouraged by others at the time of your need.

Remember, God's way is to love one another and to love thy neighbor as thy self. This is one of his commandments. This involves a lot of self-reflection and watching what you are saying. The words that you speak should always be good, and in faith should reflect how you want to be and what you want God to perform. This new language takes practice, and you will catch yourself speaking wrongly.

Think about this statement: "That person makes me sick." (You can fill in a person's name if you wish.) Your words are very powerful. The Bible states that we have the power of life and death. This power is with our tongues, and what we speak verbally. The new language you are going to learn is to speak life onto yourself and others. So when a person says that another person makes him or her sick, then in reality he or she is saying that the person can in real life make him or her sick. If this statement is said over and over, then do you not think that this is what is going to happen?

So let's take a few minutes each day and change the way we talk and think and speak good words to others and ourselves. Remember, what you say and do to others is what you ultimately receive yourself.

God's Spiritual Gifts

God has gifts for you to live a good, content life. These gifts can be described as fruit of the Spirit. The fruit of the Spirit, which we all want to receive while we are on earth and have with us at all times, is described in Galatians 5:22–23, "But the fruit of the Spirit is love, joy, peace, longsuffering, gentleness, goodness, faith, meekness, temperance."

God also has spiritual gifts for you. 1 Corinthians 14:1 states, "Follow after charity, and desire spiritual gifts, but rather that ye prophesy."

As a person of God, you are to seek and pray for spiritual gifts. You will recognize that you have one or more of them. It is a great feeling to know that God has gifts for you, to use for his glory and to build up his kingdom. Have you guessed what gift God has given to me, through the reading of this book? Always remember that when you do become aware of the gifts God has for you, they are not to be used to glorify yourself, as stated in Galatians 5:26, "Let us not be desirous of vain glory, provoking one another, envying one another."

Chapter Nine

YOUR PERSONAL GROWTH WITH GOD

PERSONAL GROWTH FOR yourself is important in getting closer to God, as he wants you closer to him. One good way to get closer to God is by removing all sin from your life. After a person has prayed to God, asking for forgiveness of a sin, and changes his or her lifestyle from the sin, God's love is able to work within him or her more freely. God's love and wisdom is now able to grow within the person. The very best way to get closer to God is to simply make him first in your life, and the desires of sin eventually go away on their own. Desire God and all of his ways as your number one priority, above all that you think and do.

To remove sin from our lives, we have to ask God for help, as we cannot do this on our own. To remove pride from your life, just ask for help. We just have to understand that God is our Father, and we are his children. We have to humble ourselves and ask for help.

If you have difficulty getting over pride in order to ask for help, then ask God to remove your pride so that you can be open to ask for help with your need to remove sin. Pray:

> Dear Father God, please remove pride from my life in the name of your Son, Jesus, and prepare me to ask for your help in removing sin from my life. Amen.

Keep praying this prayer until pride has left your life and you are able to ask God for help. Many of us are guilty of committing sins that we are not even aware of, as they are a part of our lives. Pray for forgiveness of specific things you have done that come to your mind. Ask God to open your mind to things you have done in the past that you were not aware of doing, thereby sinning without knowing it. Take a minute or two and do this. God will open your mind and tell what you have done wrong. Ask God to forgive you for these sins and to change your ways so that you won't sin any more.

Okay, now that you have asked God to forgive you for things you have done, it is time to forgive all the people in your past who have ever done anything to you. You have to release them and the negative thoughts of them. Once you release these people, ask God to fill this new void with his love, knowledge, and wisdom. Pretty cool stuff, huh? Keep out the bad stuff and bring in all the good of God's love. A person has to love God more than the sin.

I would like to share with you an experience that made an impact on me during the winter of 2002. It was a cold, wintry, dark morning, and I was on my way to work on the highway. There is a certain curve in the four lane highway that is a spiritually moving place for me. I call it Motor City curve, as there are several different car dealerships along this specific stretch of the highway. I was quite emotional and angry at the time, because it was 5:30 in the morning, and

I was not getting much sleep due to a financial situation I had gotten myself into.

Anyway, as I was driving through the curve at 55 miles an hour, I was thinking, and I angrily spoke out loud with a tear in my eye, "God, why do you make me ask for everything?" Well, I got an instant answer. God said to me in my thoughts, "Because I like to hear your voice," in a soft, loving manner. This was such a loving answer that I instantly lost my anger and thought instead of how loving an answer it was. God is so good and loving. He likes to hear my voice—yes, *my* voice—speaking to him. Wow, he made me feel good, and he also reminded me of his presence.

So I continued on to work, having this experience engrained into my mind to share with you, so you may prosper and know of his presence also. This was a powerful experience, during a time that I was down and out, knowing he is always with me.

This reminds me of another experience in which I had gone out hiking, just wanting to get away from all people and be alone. I was walking along, waiting to get a little tired and, at the same time, looking for a place to sit down and take a break. I thought I had found a place, and I sat down with my back against a pine tree, enjoying the warmth of the summer day with the smell of the pine trees, and hearing a bird chirp once in awhile. It was quiet, but I did not feel as though I was alone.

Then I moved to a spot under another tree, about two to three hundred yards from where I had just been. I just did not have a feeling of being alone. I had come to the conclusion that God's presence was there, and I would never be alone, as I always have God. I was thinking to myself that I could hike all around the world, to the far reaches of where no man is, and I still would not be alone. So I gave up trying to go hiking to be all alone. God is my partner in all that I do, and he convinced me that he is always with me, watching me, loving me, and being with me. God is always with you also; just start paying closer attention, and you, too, will see and understand his presence. If you want to be able to see and understand more of his presence, all you have to do is ask him.

Effective Prayer

Would you like to have effective prayer? God has principles by which he desires people to pray. In order for prayer to be effective, I think God wants our hearts to be prepared before we pray. The first step is to pray for forgiveness of our sins and transgressions, through the prayer of the Almighty God himself—by reciting the Lord's Prayer out loud. Here it is, for your convenience:

> Our Father which art in heaven, Hallowed be thy name. Thy kingdom come, Thy will be done in earth, as it is in heaven. Give us this day our daily bread. And forgive us our debts, as we forgive our debtors. And lead us not into temptation, but deliver us from evil: For thine is the kingdom, and the power, and the glory, for ever. Amen.

Learn this prayer by memory, and repeat it often. This is a very important prayer to know in many situations that you come into. Praying this prayer does many things for you. For one, it shows God that you are thinking of him. Second, you are praising him and honoring him by speaking his prayer.

Another prayer to confess out loud, and often, is the Apostle's Creed:

> I believe in God, the Father Almighty,
> the Creator of heaven and earth,
> and in Jesus Christ, His only Son, our Lord:

Who was conceived of the Holy Spirit,
born of the Virgin Mary,
suffered under Pontius Pilate,
was crucified, died, and was buried.
He descended into hell.
The third day He arose again from the dead.

He ascended into heaven
and sits at the right hand of God the Father Almighty,
whence He shall come to judge the living and the dead.

I believe in the Holy Spirit, the holy catholic church,
the communion of saints,
the forgiveness of sins,
the resurrection of the body,
and life everlasting. Amen.

The Nicene Creed is also a good prayer to pray and confess out loud and often:

> I believe in one God, the Father Almighty, Maker of heaven and earth, and of all things visible and invisible.
>
> And in one Lord Jesus Christ, the only-begotten Son of God, begotten of the Father before all worlds; God of God, Light of Light, very God of very God; begotten, not made, being of one substance with the Father, by whom all things were made.
>
> Who, for us men and for our salvation, came down from heaven, and was incarnate by the Holy Spirit of the virgin Mary, and was made man; and was crucified also for us under Pontius Pilate; He suffered and was buried; and the third day He rose again, according to the Scriptures; and ascended into heaven, and sits on the right hand of the Father; and He shall come again, with glory, to judge the quick and the dead; whose kingdom shall have no end.

And I believe in the Holy Ghost, the Lord and Giver of Life; who proceeds from the Father and the Son; who with the Father and the Son together is worshipped and glorified; who spoke by the prophets.

And I believe in one holy catholic and apostolic Church. I acknowledge one baptism for the remission of sins; and I look for the resurrection of the dead, and the life of the world to come. Amen.

When I say these prayers out loud, the Holy Spirit comes onto me and sends chills up and down my back (and sometimes the backs of my legs), and just loves me and shows me that this is true, to communicate with me. It is happening even now, as I write this, because he loves you so much and wants you to know this so very much, so he can also love you. Thank you, Lord God. Amen.

Pray to God in the name of Jesus the Christ, heavenly Father, and through the shed blood of Jesus. I believe that saying the name of Jesus is powerful and gives authority on earth for God. Colossians 3:17 states, "And whatsoever ye do in word or deed, do all in the name of the Lord Jesus, giving thanks to God the Father by him." Also, John 14:13 says, "And whatsoever ye shall ask in my name, that will I do, that the Father may be glorified in the Son." I make it a habit to always start out all of my prayers in this manner.

Luke 10:17 states, "And the seventy returned again with joy, saying, Lord, even the devils are subject unto us through thy name." This is again referring to the name of Jesus and the power of that five-letter name. It is the name above all names. Also, the book of 1 Peter, chapter 3, verse 22 refers to Jesus after his resurrection, "Who is gone into heaven, and is on the right hand of God; angels and authorities and powers being made subject unto him."

The words of the Bible are to speak for themselves, as they are written by the hand of man, from the Holy Spirit, who speaks through us. So to provide spiritual authority in prayer, I prefer to start all my prayers with "in the name of Jesus." I also interject "the blood of Jesus," as this is a reminder that Satan was defeated when Jesus died on the cross and rose again. There is a lot of authority in blood, as it gives every living creature life. And through the sacrament of Holy Communion, Jesus' body and blood is our reminder of his victory over Satan.

Pray for forgiveness for your recent and past sins committed against people who are in your lives on a daily basis. Meditate or think for a minute, and God will put on your heart how you should pray for people who need to forgive you. Then visualize them forgiving you for what you have done to them.

Many times it is well worth calling the people to apologize and simply asking them to forgive you for what you have done. Ask God also to forgive you for what you have done to them, and ask God to show you who you need to forgive. Forgiveness is very important. Genesis 50:17 says, "So shall ye say unto Joseph, Forgive, I pray thee now, the trespass of thy brethren, and their sin; for they did unto thee evil: and now, we pray thee, forgive the trespass of the servants of the God of thy father. And Joseph wept when they spake unto him."

Next, pray in an unselfish way that will glorify God and expand his kingdom. Selfish prayer will not be answered, as stated in James 4:3, "Ye ask, and receive not, because ye ask amiss, that ye may consume it upon your lusts."

During your prayer, tell God—and mean it from deep inside your heart and spirit—how you love him, and praise him and honor him for the blessing of being his servant.

1 Thessalonians 5:18 says, "In everything give thanks: for this is the will of God in Christ Jesus concerning you."

It is important to bind the negative things in your path and to pray that these are bound in the name and shed blood of Jesus. Then pray for protection of God's holy, warring angels against these influences. Matthew 16:19 says, "And I will give unto thee the keys of the kingdom of heaven: and whatsoever thou shalt bind on earth shall be bound in heaven: and whatsoever thou shalt loose on earth shall be loosed in heaven."

Pray the prayer as if your request has already happened. James 1:6 states, "But let him ask in faith, nothing wavering. For he that wavereth is like a wave of the sea driven with the wind and tossed." Also Matthew 21:22 states, "And all things, whatsoever ye shall ask in prayer, believing, you will receive." Know in faith that you have already received your request from God.

Quote God's principles to him as you pray with others. Matthew 18:19 says, "Again I say unto you, That if two of you shall agree on earth as touching any thing that they shall ask, it shall be done for them of my Father which is in heaven." When praying with other people, and someone is praying out loud, verbally state your agreement with them in a low voice.

Be joyful and happy in your prayers, believing that you have already received what you asked for. This is easier to do than you think. It is just a different way of understanding how God works. "For my thoughts are not your thoughts, neither are your ways my ways, saith the Lord" (Isaiah 55:8). His ways are not the way we do things, so we need to get into tune with the way he does things.

The concept here is to know in faith what you want to happen, and sing in happiness and joy for what you are about to receive. Second Chronicles, chapter 20, verse 22 says, "And when they began to sing and to praise, the Lord set ambushments against the children of Ammon, Moab, and mount Se-ir which were come against Judah; and they were smitten." To me, this means that our singing and praising for what is needed shows a powerful faith of expectation that God is victorious in your moment of need. Accept nothing else but victory. 1Thessalonians 5:16 states, "Rejoice evermore." This includes during prayer and your daily activities.

Be specific in your prayer. Use as much description and as many adjectives as possible, always remembering that the prayer must glorify God, his ways, and his kingdom.

Continuously pray throughout the day. First Thessalonians, chapter 5, verse 17 states, "Pray without ceasing." Always conclude your prayer by saying, "Amen."

Fasting for Effective Prayer

If you wish your prayer to be magnified, then you should consider fasting. Fasting is going without something, like food. When a person sacrifices something, such as food or an activity that he or she really enjoys, it will teach that person that the habit is a type of addiction. Selfishness plays a big role in habits and addictions. Most of the time it will consume the person's time and efforts. This is a weapon that the devil uses to keep us busy from serving and learning about God. When we begin to start focusing on other people's needs and set our wants aside, our hearts will soften.

When a person performs a fast from something, he or she should do it with the right frame of mind, remembering that the act of fasting is for the glory of God and his purpose. The definition of a fast is going without the chewing and eating of solid food. No sugar of any type is allowed, as it will induce hunger pains. Drinking fluids, such as a vitamin drink, is okay (without sugar, of course). The concept of fasting is so very important. The fasting clears the mind for hearing God, and at the same time, you are saying to God that he is first in your life, and food is taking a backseat and is no longer number one in your life.

I am praising you for taking this step to honor God, in which you are complying with the first commandment. Please keep fasting in mind when you or another person need clarity, direction, and understanding of God's ways; however, please seek medical advice, direction, and monitoring before attempting this.

Your body needs liquid nutrients during a fast. Drink lots of water. Pray every moment you can, binding the devil when you pray out loud, and praising God, talking to him as your best friend when you pray quietly to yourself. Read the Bible while you are fasting. Clarity and understanding will come while you are fasting.

Loving Your Neighbor

The number one thing I find people need to focus on, as Christians, is to "love thy neighbor as thyself," which is the second greatest commandment. The first and second greatest commandments are first and second in God's mind for a reason, so focus, focus, and focus. I am guilty of not loving my neighbor as myself, and I am finding ways to make myself more aware of this. I seek ways to better myself. Consider that you may want to find ways also, by looking at yourself for improvements, watching how others do this, or reading books.

The selfish way of the world has to be set aside for this concept to sink in. People need to learn to speak to and treat others in the way they want to be treated!

Baptism

God wants all his children to be baptized with water and the Holy Ghost. If you have not been baptized with water, seek out a church and ask the pastor to set up a time for a water baptism for you. Do not let any negative thoughts keep you from doing this, and just make it happen. God would like all people to receive his Spirit. One may ask a pastor to pray with them to receive the Holy Ghost, as it states in Acts 1:5.

People go through baby steps in getting closer to God, so as thirsty as you are to get as close to God as fast as you can, be patient, and enjoy the love and knowledge of the teaching along the path. This is an awesome experience, as you walk in and learn God's ways. It is so powerful to be engulfed with all his love so that you may share it with others. In Acts 1:5 it talks about being baptized in the Holy Ghost, "For John truly baptized with water, but ye shall be baptized with the Holy Ghost not many days hence." Ask for this specific baptism when you are ready to receive the fullness of the Holy Ghost.

During this writing, God spoke to me, to tell you that I was to type the words for him, and he will come onto the hearts of the readers, to deliver what they need at the time. Just put down the words, and he will take care of the rest. So be assured he is speaking to you, once you have prepared your heart for him. God bless you, my brother and sister! He is talking to you; just listen to your heart for his loving words to you in his quiet, loving voice. God speaks to your spirit as though there is a transference of his knowledge to you, so his knowledge comes to you as if you just know something. He does not just speak to you.

Christian Resources

If a person ever wants more information on something in particular, or simply anything at all in growing with God, all a person has to do is go to a Christian bookstore and ask for help to find what he or she needs. The Bible is obviously the first place to go to learn about God's Word and his ways. However, supplemental information can be acquired on the internet and in books ordered from an online bookstore. We are in the information age, and acquiring information is very easy through the computer. Getting information from sources other than the Bible allows a person to gain understanding from another person about what God wants us to know and understand.

All you have to do is think of something you want to learn, and make an inquiry using a search engine on the internet, and you can find anything you want. Being a person who is thirsty for knowledge to get closer to God, go out and seek what God has for you, and have fun while doing it. Smile. God loves you!

Chapter Ten

HOW TO GROW WITH YOUR CHURCH

THE FIRST THING that comes to mind concerning how to grow with your church is that all the people of the church body are an extension of God, which is in essence the Holy Trinity of the Father, the Son (Jesus), and the Holy Spirit. We are all God's children, therefore, being an extension of the church body. 1 Corinthians 12:12 says, "For as the body is one, and hath many members, and all members of that one body, being many, are one body: so also is Christ."

The Unity of Believers

Above all, when there are people involved, God wants you and the church body to be united. This should be the foremost direction for you and the leadership of the church. To accomplish this mission, it is very important to pray in agreement with each other—in unity, for God's ultimate glory of loving each other in the very best way that we know how, and in reading, understanding, and applying God's principles based in the Bible.

God wants and demands unity in all churches. The opposite of unity is division, which is opposition to God's ways. People are more loving when all the people of the church are treating others with God's love. This love attracts other people to want to come to church and to want to be around this spirit. This spirit is God, as God is love.

Growing in Christ is based on the love each and every person has for his fellow man. When people have the love of God within and share it with others, churches grow in knowledge and in numbers. People are attracted by the love other individuals have within themselves and how they share it with others.

When division comes into the congregation, this should be prayed against immediately—pray for unity, agreement, and to praise God for all the blessings the church has had bestowed upon it. Matthew 18:18 says, "Verily I say unto you, Whatsoever ye shall bind on earth shall be bound in heaven: and whatsoever ye shall loose on earth shall be loosed in heaven."

The evil spirit of division, also named "the strongman," has accompanying spirits that help to accomplish the division. The strongman, in my interpretation, can be any core or main motivating evil spirit that is blinding or controlling a person or group. This can be an evil, critical spirit, along with hatred, envy, unbelief, or others. This is a very important principle to remember as you grow with God.

Love and Encouragement

Love and encouragement are very contagious. Loving people build others up, support others, and take care of others. The church body, comprised of the membership of the church, is basically an extension of one's family. They are your brothers and sisters in Christ—a unique group of people that you bond with in God's love, through the Holy Spirit. Many times when I meet someone, I feel as though I have known that person for years. What I recognize is love, and that love comes from God. It is a great feeling within myself to sense the love within someone else.

God's love is universal. Everyone can experience love for others. It is just that today it seems people are careful how God's love for others is shared. As each member of the church body grows closer to God, he or she becomes fruitful by bearing fruit and becoming more prosperous. This, therefore, prospers the church body. By fruitful, I mean that the person enjoys the full fruit of the Spirit, as stated in Galatians 5:22, "But the fruit of the Spirit is love, joy, peace, longsuffering, gentleness, goodness, faith, meekness, temperance: against such there is no law." This is achieved by remembering what is said in Galatians 5:14, "For all the law is fulfilled in one word, even in this; Thou shalt love thy neighbor as thyself."

Giving to Others

Being considerate of one another and offering to help in whatever needs to be done is so very important. When you sense within yourself that you have nothing to give, this is the time to give. This is the time that God wants you to have faith and to give when you feel as though you have nothing to give, or even the desire to give. This is when God wants you to give; this allows selfishness to be set aside, and love of your fellow man to take priority. This is when God knows you are his and you are getting closer to him. Remember that Isaiah 55:8 says, "For my thoughts are not your thoughts, neither are your ways my ways, saith the Lord."

Share whatever you have with others. Too often, when someone is in need, people run the other way. I, too, was once this way. I did not understand what I needed to do to help someone, so I went the other way. I should have just asked the person in need, "What can I do to help you?" without giving up. Asking the person what I can do to help is of value. Maybe just being present is all that is needed. Just think: what if the church was there to lend a helping hand every time someone needed help? Would this be the ideal church? Yes, it would, but it may not be realistic.

Pray for Each Other

Many times we learn from the hard knocks that God sends our way. God gets our attention so that we may persevere and ultimately get closer to him. This also strengthens our prayer life. Pray for others when you see a possible weakness that you think God can strengthen. In the same prayer, ask God to strengthen you in this very same way.

Ask for congregational prayer for the leadership of your very own church, that the leadership would be protected by God's love, along with asking for prayer from any prayer groups that are praying for others. Strong prayer warriors need backup prayer groups to be praying for them. Join one of these groups to learn about prayer and God's love through prayer. All the time, keep in mind that, in the spiritual world, there is a battle for your mind, to control your thoughts and actions. Strong prayer and recognition of this is important to stay on the path of God's ways. A good prayer includes saying the name of Jesus in a prayer to God, believing in faith that what we pray for will happen, and binding possible negative things from the devil that may influence the positive outcome of the prayer.

With your mouth and tongue, speak good words unto others always, for you are planting seeds of goodness to other people. I was in a spiritual fellowship meeting with a group of men several months ago, and one of the men prophesied over me, to pray for a crop failure of the bad seeds that I have planted in my life and in other people's lives.

This can also be applied to churches. To pray as a group in unity for a crop failure of the bad seeds planted within the church. Pray for the seeds left over from the trials the church has been through and that these seeds would be replanted with God's love and for a bountiful harvest for the church. The church body is to pray forgiveness and blessing upon people who have caused grief. It is Satan and his ways that cause the grief, and we should bind the strongman.

Tithing

We have talked about tithing money to God's work in an earlier chapter. Tithing is a blessing of knowledge of one of God's principles of giving. I call it a blessing because it is a blessing to know this, as I was not aware of this knowledge and the importance of it until I was in my late forties. This is passed down from your parents, or possibly from your church body, or even a brother or sister in Christ.

By giving money cheerfully, without wanting anything in return, you show both yourself and God that money is not ruling your life, and God is. I think that by tithing, you turn your spending over to God, and therefore, he is in charge. This helps a person and family manage finances and gives wisdom on how to stretch the budget to be more fruitful. Understand this principle, and believe in faith that it is true. If you are challenged by this, ask God with the following prayer:

> Dear heavenly Father, through your strength I praise you, and thank you for giving me the wisdom and personal strength to follow you and keep you first over money. Allow me to understand your principle of giving what I expect to receive. Open my mind, body, and spirit to this concept. Thank you, Lord. Amen.

Obey God's Commandments

One of the main ways to grow in Christ or in God's love is to observe and obey the Ten Commandments. Secondly, to grow in Christ is to be observant of your behavior, and to restrain and rid your self of any feelings of jealousy, hatred, anger, control of people or situations, manipulation of people or situations, adultery, fornication, uncleanness, idolatry, witchcraft, wrath, strife, envying, murdering, drunkenness, covetousness, ungodliness, dishonoring your own or someone else's body, homosexuality, being plain mean to your fellow man, deceit, backstabbing your fellow man, hating God, being proud, being boastful, being disobedient to one's parents or authority, lacking in mercy, being greedy, lustful, desiring revenge, inflicting pain on others (either physical or emotional), using drugs, pornography, and selfishness. In Galatians 5:19–21 it states:

> Now the works of the flesh are manifest, which are these; Adultery, fornication, uncleanness, lasciviousness, idolatry, witchcraft, hatred, variance, emulations, wrath, strife, seditions, heresies, envying, murders, drunkenness, revellings, and such like: of the which I tell you before, as I have also told you in time past, that they which do such things shall not inherit the kingdom of God.

If these become a primary motivation for a person, there are usually two or more other emotions that are helpers. Getting rid of the desire for the primary motivation is the secret to conquering the feeling or emotion. This is done by persistently asking God to remove the emotion or feeling until it is all gone. Sometimes you need someone to pray for you, to help to remove the desire for the emotion or feeling. Once you accept that the feeling or emotion needs to go and is controlling your life, ask for peace and to be delivered from this bondage so you may become free. Start out by asking God:

> Dear God, through your Son, Jesus, I pray to you to please strengthen me and to take away these feelings of ______, as I do need your help and cannot do this on my own. Thank you for removing these feelings and replacing these bad feelings with good, loving feelings and emotions of being filled with love from the Holy Spirit. Amen.

Once this is done, remove all items or materials that have anything to do with the bad behavior. Look for a transformation to take place immediately, or even up to three days later. This transformation will result in an immediate, newfound peace of being delivered from your old ways. Now you have a new strength to also avoid the circumstances that led unto the bad behavior. When the old desire does come about, just ask God, in the name of Jesus, for the desire to go away. It is as easy as that. Thank God very often for your deliverance from your captivity.

So to review: ask to be delivered, expect to be delivered, ask for a transformation, and expect a transformation and change in behavior. Focus on obtaining the fruit of the Spirit. Join a Bible study that meets weekly, and read the

Bible daily. Become a member of a church. Learn as much as you can about love and God's ways.

Christian Education

One of the ways that I like to learn about God is by going to a Christian bookstore and buying different books from different authors on topics I am interested in. Authors are gifted in God's grace to communicate something specific God wants people to know and learn about. Read, understand, learn, and apply the newfound knowledge.

Once you do learn something new, it now becomes your way of living to share this newfound love and knowledge of God with others. God will give you a divine appointment with someone who is open to learn this knowledge, which you will deliver in a very loving way unto your Christian brother or sister. Before you go to a Bible study, a church service, your work, your recreational play, or a simple meeting with someone, pray that God will bless the meeting or activity, and that you will represent him in a manner which is pleasing to him.

A couple of years ago, I was doing some electrical work for a very strong spiritual lady by the name of Marge, who is a close neighbor of my parents. While I was working, she asked me a question. She said, "Robin, do you pray for your work?" I stated no, I did not, and she said, "You should always pray for your work." I said I had not really thought about it. Ever since that day, I make an effort to pray for my work, and I lovingly think of her. What a blessing to hear this strong, good advice. Just recently I asked her if she remembered the day she gave me this good advice, and she said, "No, I do not remember; it must have been the Holy Spirit." I believe it was the Holy Spirit, talking through her to me. Thank you, Lord God, for this word of knowledge.

I share this experience with you so that you may see how the Holy Spirit works through others. She influenced my life by encouraging me to pray for my daily work activities. She did not take credit for it, but she gave credit to the Holy Spirit. So now, dear reader, I ask you to pray continually for your work and activities.

When people thank me for something, I ask them to thank God, as I am a servant of God. I do not like to take credit for what I do, as God has given me the gifts that he wants me to have, to work and to serve others in their time of need.

Volunteer

Think about this for a minute. God has given you gifts to serve others, also. Make use of those gifts in the church body by helping out in the church or your community. Volunteer to help with whatever is necessary. It could be your time, your intelligence, your finances, or your expertise. Everyone is good at something. Go on and take the first step, and call the church or community in which you live, then volunteer. Be bold, and just do it. Go in faith, and pray that God will help you to learn new ways to help people with your services. Once you do, you will feel really good about helping others.

Do not ask for anything in return for your services, or brag about how you have helped people. God knows. The blessing is in giving from your heart. Through your giving, you invoke God's spiritual principles of sowing and reaping. Luke 6:38 says:

> Give, and it shall be given unto you; good measure, pressed down, and shaken together, and running over, shall men give into your bosom. For with the same

measure that ye mete withal it shall be measured to you again.

It feels good to give of yourself with what you have, remembering that God determines the time to give. So when the opportunity comes to give to someone, jump on it with lots of energy and give. The opportunity may not come again in this particular situation. So take advantage of the situation, and give of your time, talents, or finances. God is testing you to see if you are listening. You listen with your heart, as God is love and lives in your heart.

Living by God's Principles

God's principles govern our everyday life whether we are aware of it or not. Once a person understands all the principles, life is much easier and more joyful. To understand all the concepts of the principles, all a person has to do is to ask God for understanding and explanation, and in time, these will be provided. Sometimes the answers are given instantly, and other times it takes a little longer. It just depends on what God thinks you need at that moment. Know in faith that the answers will come.

This is very important to understand: the principles of God are a way of life, from minute to minute, throughout a person's lifetime and into eternity. All words of God in the Bible are very powerful. Many times there are people within a group who have the God-given gift of discernment, who can recognize the different works of God and of the devil, to bring to light what may be happening. Search for such a person, and ask for his or her opinion once in awhile, if he or she doesn't voice it. Work with this concept, but do not dwell much on the dark side, to give it too much attention; instead, remain positive with the love of God.

Chapter Eleven

GOD'S AUDIBLE VOICE SAVES MY LIFE

GOD SAVES MANY lives everyday, so what makes it so special that God saved my life? I thought the way in which God saved my life was very special. You will also see how it is unique, and how it can apply to you, as the reader, to be encouraged with God's presence and power.

I should give you some background on how God saved my life and show you how he wanted me closer to him. Telling you how he saved my life will give you some physical proof (myself) of a spiritual entity (God) who is an almighty, powerful, omnipotent, omnipresent force, and the ruler of this earth and the heavens.

To begin with, I should mention that I am an avid outdoorsman and a person who enjoys the time-honored American tradition of hunting majestic elk in the Rocky Mountains of Colorado. This prepares you for the background of the spiritual event that occurred in December of 2002. I had been planning an elk hunt with my son (who was 14 at the time), a friend of his, and another group of 2 boys and an adult. We planned to return to a place where

Ryan (my son) had successfully hunted just two years prior. Considering the cold weather at this time of year, we had to bring lots of warm clothes. With the three of us traveling in a SUV, I had decided to bring along a covered trailer to store equipment that we might need for the trip.

The night before we left, Ryan and I scurried around, gathering up all the gear we were going to need for the hunting/camping trip. We started by putting all the gear in our living room, as a staging area, until we actually loaded it into the vehicle. We usually have a list of gear we need, so we can check off the items as we pack them into the car. This time was no exception. We packed away a couple of sleeping bags to keep us warm, as though we were between two pieces of hot toast just out of the toaster. We were expecting it to get below freezing during the night, and we didn't want to be the ones frozen like an ice cube in the freezer.

Rosie, being a good mother and wife, always helps us out with our hunger by having some fresh apples and a pumpkin pie to snack on while we are out in the field. She knows that we get into a hurry and do not always pack snacks, so she also buys us some other goodies to take with us. After a hard day of hiking in snow and cold, carrying a ten-pound day pack on our backs, wearing heavy boots and heavy clothes, the aroma of pumpkin pie always brings us back to civilization. The taste of whipped cream on the pie is the ultimate flavor to the taste buds.

Two years prior, Ryan and I hiked 7 miles on a hunting trip, 2 and 1/2 of those miles in the dark, with temperatures in the low teens. So the snacks always come in handy, as they are readily available quick energy. Most of the time we just cut a piece of pie, put on the whipped cream with a spoon, and eat it like finger food or a sandwich with our hands. Yum!

Once we had loaded everything we could think of into our SUV (sports utility vehicle), all we had to do is grab our toothbrushes and items in the refrigerator. Then we laid our heads on our pillows to get some sleep before we headed out. When the radio alarm clock went off early Friday morning, at the crisp hour of 4:30 A.M., I turned on the hallway light and walked into Ryan's room to wake him. He moved his legs, and moaned a little, sleepily acknowledging it was time to get up. I went downstairs, turned on the furnace to warm the house up a few degrees, and turned on a few more lights. As we got dressed, I started to feel excitement building up inside me, looking forward to the fellowship of everyone's company over the short weekend. Rose got up also and helped make sure we remembered to pack everything.

Before we leave on any trip, we always gather in the front room and pray. Joining hands, we thank God for all of our blessings, and we ask for safety and protection for all of us while we are separated, speaking what is on our hearts in agreement and unity.

When our prayer ended, we said our goodbyes, and Ryan and I went out to the car, ready to go pick up Ryan's friend. As we drove off, Rose waved goodbye to us, standing in the doorway of our house.

It was a dark and crispy cold morning on the streets of Colorado Springs as we headed to the north end of town to pick up Ryan's friend. He lives in a cul-de-sac and, with a trailer behind me, I decided not to go up the long driveway, but instead, I pulled up in front of the drive. Ryan ran up to the house, and the two guys come back with some hunting gear. His mother came down the long driveway to see us off. We greeted each other with good morning salutations and a little chit chat while the boys put gear into the Jeep and trailer.

During the conversation, the mother expressed her concern about the safety of her son with the other youth that were going, all having rifles, and that we should be extra careful. This gave me a red flag, as I know that mothers have a sixth sense about things, and I knew I should be careful. I assured her that, when we got together with the other group, I would conduct a safety briefing with reminders so that we would have a safe hunting experience. We then joined hands in prayer behind the trailer, said our goodbyes, and then off we went.

It was about 6 A.M. when we left, and six hours later, we were at the camp site, looking for the other guys that we were to meet. There were no signs in the snow that they were even there. We looked around; we were the only ones there. I recalled the directions we had talked about, and I remembered that we were to meet at the windmill.

We wanted to do a little hunting before it got dark. We still had about 4 hours of daylight, so we set up the tent rather quickly, on top of 3–4 inches of snow, and put the sleeping gear and the propane heater into the tent for some warmth later on. This was an opportunity to see if we could find the other guys too, while we went out to see if we could find some elk.

We were traveling down a dirt road, about 15 miles from camp, next to a river, when we saw a dead elk lying down in an alfalfa field about a hundred yards from the road. Elk have two ivory teeth that are commonly used for jewelry, rings, and necklaces, and I thought it would be a good idea to go on down to the animal to see if the ivory teeth were still in place. Many people will come along and remove the ivory teeth, just as I was thinking to do.

From a distance, the elk looked as though it had not been there a very long time, as there were no signs that any animals or birds were in the area, and there was no evidence of any critters nibbling on the carcass.

I stopped the car on the two lane dirt road and said to the boys, "Let's go on down there to see if the elk still has its ivories." They said okay, so we all went down to the elk. We did have an obstacle though, and that was to cross over a three-strand barbed wire fence, which went okay.

The cow elk did still have the ivory teeth, and we acted as though we were skilled dentists, adding two more ivory teeth to our collection. Crossing over the barbed wire fence on the way back, Ryan snagged his blue jeans on one of the barbs and tore his lower leg open with a pretty good gash. He was bleeding, so we performed some first aid. He still has a long, 3-inch scar. Thinking back, I don't think the ivory teeth were worth the wound, but hindsight is always 20/20, isn't it?

We got back to the car, looked for the other guys, and decided to go back to camp, get something to eat, and go to bed. We played checkers and chess while warming up the tent with the propane heater. We did finally go to bed, only to wake up to about half an inch of fresh, white snow. Looking around, I was hoping the guys had come through the night and set up camp close to us, but this was not the case. I turned on the propane heater in the tent so the guys would be warm when they got up. It was still dark out though, as it was only 5 A.M.

The heater started melting the frost inside the tent. Climbing out of their warm, toasty sleeping bags, the boys got dressed into some warm clothes, anticipating a cold day. We turned everything off, zipped up the tent, and left in the Jeep to see if we could find the other guys, and find some elk.

We were about 10 miles from camp when we spotted a herd of 30 elk, about 2 miles away, in a huge field. There were some other hunters who were closer to them than we were, and we decided to just watch what was going on for a little while. After 15 minutes had gone by, I decided to see if we could go up the paved road so the boys could possibly get a shot. So we drove 5–6 miles west of where we had previously seen the elk, and then took a dirt road, coming around to where I thought the elk might be.

There was no sign of any herd of elk when we reached the top of a high vantage point. We could see a long distance, and there were absolutely no trees in sight, just rolling hills, covered with fresh, cold, wet snow. We could see open country for miles, but no elk. To describe the terrain, I would have to say that there were no scrub oak and no trees, just hill after hill. I am used to being in the mountains with lots of ponderosa pine, blue spruce, and aspen trees.

We were traveling in my four-wheel-drive Jeep along two-track roads, which are basically dirt roads with grass growing between the tire tracks. We were traveling about 3–4 miles from a paved road, and there were no people around. It was a quiet morning. We were not seeing many birds. The sun was shining, and it was pretty crisp out, around 30-some degrees would be my guess. It was just a beautiful winter day, with the sun glistening off the newly fallen snow.

We started heading up a fairly steep hill, which I actually had second thoughts about going up, as it was kind of steep. I thought to myself that if we started slipping, I would just back up, make a turn into the hill, and go back down, as it was so open, with no trees. We started going up the hill and did not have any trouble at all, as we were making tracks in the snow, and on the way back, I would simply put the Jeep into the very lowest gear so the vehicle would not slide down the hill.

We got to the top, and now we were traveling on a ridge line, where we could see down both sides into little gullies here and there. We had a good view, being on top of a high point. On the left side, down in one of the gullies, I had spotted an elk without antlers that was lying down about 250 yards away. I stopped and told the boys to grab their rifles, and let's go see if the elk still had its ivory teeth. So we got out of the car, and the boys grabbed their rifles from the back of the car and loaded them up, making sure that the safety was on so that they would not fire on their own if the trigger was pulled or pushed by accident. We closed the hatch on the rear of the car and started our short hike to the cow elk.

It is always a good practice, when hunting, to take a firearm with you, as you just never know if an animal that you have a license for will appear within shooting distance. As we walked towards the elk, we were all walking side by side, with my son Ryan on my left, and his friend on my right. Ryan was carrying a 30 caliber rifle, known as a 30-06 with a rifle scope, and his friend was carrying my rifle, which is a 300 Weatherby magnum and scope. This is a 30 caliber bullet, but with a lot more gunpowder in the casing, which provides for more power and distance.

We were walking and talking a little, like hunters do, and I did not realize it, but time was slowing down for me. This is a strange situation that has happened to me before, and I am beginning to understand it. It is very similar to an adrenaline rush to the brain. However, I did not feel as though there was a reason for an adrenaline rush at the time. I was thinking to myself that it had snowed last night, and there was no snow on the top of the elk, so it had not been there that long. I knew something was peculiar; possibly there were hunters around who had shot this elk just as it expired. I just thought that we would go check things out and retrieve the ivories, as we had done the day before.

The elk was facing away from us, facing down the hill. When we were about 100 yards away from the animal, guess what happened? Yup, it got up and started running away from us. However, it was running away with a limp in its rear leg. I knew we were meant to come across this animal, so the meat could be used by us, and so we could take its pain and suffering away by harvesting it within the next few minutes. It was just a matter of time until we would catch up, as we no doubt had an advantage.

I was still bewildered by why it did not get up and run when we stopped the car, as surely we had made some noise that it could hear. Remember, I am feeling as though I am in a time warp, and what I consider a spiritual-type fog. In the winter of 2005, God told me in a dream that he controls time. I can accept that, as God is the most powerful force on the planet, and in the entire universe, for that matter. He said it, so I believe it. It is as simple as that. God is omnipotent and omnipresent. He knows everything, is everywhere, and surrounds us.

As the elk was running away from us, I gave verbal instructions to the boys to shoot the elk. Ryan was to my immediate left, within a few feet of me. I remember feeling like a proud Dad as Ryan had been blessed with harvesting an elk last year, and now he was shouldering the rifle, looking through the scope and about to harvest one this year, too. An average hunter harvests an elk about once every 10 years, and some people who have been hunting all their life have never harvested an elk.

Being the type of person I am, I told Ryan to hold up and not shoot, to let his friend harvest the elk, as he had never done so. This would be a good, humane opportunity to harvest the wounded elk. The injured elk would not live long in the wild, and it could possibly be eaten alive by coyotes. I knew God meant for us to be there at that very minute in time.

As I was observing the unfolding events, a thought came to my mind to step to the right. I asked myself, "Why do I want to move to the right?" I was feeling the proud parent emotion, and I was not done enjoying the moment. In the meantime, Ryan took the rifle down from his shoulder and was holding it in front of him. I did not realize that Ryan's friend had fallen behind us about 10 feet as we were walking along. Since I had received instructions from my mind to "step to the right," I started thinking about how I should move: should I side step, or should I pivot around to my right. Just after I received these thoughts in my mind, I heard a very loud but firm voice say, "DON'T MOVE." I was literally a little scared, but I listened and was not about to move after getting this type of an instruction. With my eyes and mouth wide open, and feeling fearful and breathless like a small child responding to a concerned, commanding parent, I said, "OKAY, OKAY, I WON'T MOVE!" I said it to myself, obediently and very loudly, like a son responding to his Father speaking with authority. I knew it was Father God. There was absolutely no doubt in my mind at all; I knew the voice was from God himself.

In the Bible it says something like, "my sheep know my voice." Being one of God's sheep, I knew his voice very distinctly. John 10:4, 27 says, "And when he putteth forth his own sheep, he goeth before them, and the sheep follow him: for they know his voice ... My sheep hear my voice, and I know them, and they follow me."

Within a split second of hearing the voice of God, I heard Ryan's friend shoot my rifle. He was behind me and to my right. If I had side-stepped, I would have been shot in the back, and if I had pivoted, I would have been shot in the chest. As the adult, I was ultimately responsible and should have been more attentive to what was going on.

I have thought about this many times, and I know for a fact that Satan can put thoughts in a person's mind; however, he cannot read a person's mind. Satan watches a person's actions and keeps him or her busy doing everything but God's work. This is his job, using deception, lying, and everything he can use to keep a person from doing God's work. Think about that for a minute; it is a very powerful statement. As an example, I have just given you a story showing this very same thing.

First of all, Satan put the thought into my mind to step to the right. Then my mind starting thinking how I was going to move, but God stepped in and gave me an audible voice to hear him. This story involves three different entities: God, the devil, and a person's mind. Understand this, because this is very important to understand.

The devil is always putting thoughts into our minds. It is up to you to decide if it is your thought or not. If it is bad (does not agree with the Bible), then it cannot be of God, and it is more than likely not yours, so it must be that of the devil. This thought has to be instantly renounced, in the name of Jesus, to make it go away. As individuals, we have to deal with our thoughts, with the devil's input as thoughts, and with God's voice as he communicates with our spirit. We do not always hear the audible voice, but we have to do what is right and go on with how our heart tells us to act. God is in our hearts, and that is where love is. God is love in its purest form. Everything that is done with love is serving God.

God did not allow Satan to take my life, for there is a Bible passage in which I see proof that God was protecting me, and it follows the passage of "My sheep hear my voice, and I know them, and they follow me." Being one of God's sheep, I knew his voice very distinctly. In the book of John, chapter 10, verses 4 and 27, it says, "And I gave unto them eternal life; and they shall never perish, neither shall any man pluck them out of my hand."

What I get out of this statement is that God was not going to allow a human being to take my life, especially if Satan were to influence the act as he did by putting the thoughts into my head of stepping in front of a shooting rifle. When the reality of almost being shot came to my mind during those moments, I was in shock and disbelief at the occurrence. I never thought in my wildest dreams that this type of thing would happen to me.

Within a few minutes of hearing the voice of God, I asked Ryan and his friend if they heard the voice of instruction, and both of them said no. There is a story in the Bible, in 1 Samuel 3, about two brothers, one of whom hears the audible voice of God when it comes upon Samuel. This is an example of hearing the audible voice, and also there is a chapter that talks about the audible voice where in the time of crisis a person may hear the voice, which was what happened to me in this crisis situation.

The cow elk was harvested within minutes by Ryan's friend. The elk hunt resulted in providing big game meat along with fellowship of friends in the history honored tradition of hunting.

This is no doubt a spiritual experience that I will never forget, and I thank Ryan and his friend for this experience, so that I may share it with you. I thank God for his love for me, and for saving my life by intervening and even showing me and the world his power. I realize that the spiritual fog that I was in was being in the hand of God himself. How grateful I am to be protected like this. God has more work for me to do to serve him, and I am so glad to share with you some instances of his holy presence throughout this book.

Chapter Twelve

GOD IS IN CONTROL

ACCEPTING AND INVITING Jesus into your heart is the first and most important step a person can take in his or her life. This is the first step in growing with God and a big turning point in a person's spiritual life. Essentially, when a person turns his or her life over to God through his Son, Jesus, he or she is submitting to allowing God to control his or her life. This is very difficult for those who are used to controlling their own lives. Every day we have the ability to control different things that we do. However, we are to submit control of our lives to God. We can fight, stomp up and down, and do whatever we want, but when God has hold of a person, that person will give up sooner or later, and must submit to God.

I did this and just said to God, "God, I give up. I know you are in charge. Show me what you want me to do." A controlling evil spirit is hard to break, but I will let you know from personal experience that God knows how to get your attention with what you think is important. God will take it away to let you know that it really is not that important. He is to be number one in your life, and you are to love your neighbor as yourself. These are the two greatest commandments, and though the principles of his laws are not obeyed, God will keep challenging you until you obey him. If you decide not to obey him, then you are to accept the consequences as of your own fault and doing.

It's Your Choice

So now that you are aware of two of the most important commandments, you are ultimately responsible for things that happen in your life. God gives us a personal choice to daily live a blessed life in following his ways; otherwise, we are subject to the ways of the devil. People live either a blessed life or a cursed life of the world, going from struggle to struggle. Which one do you want? I would prefer to have a blessed, joyful, and peaceful life.

We live by our own choices. Our lives are either blessed or they are cursed. What kind of life do you live, dear reader? Is it a life you are happy with? If it's not the life that you want, then you have the right to make a decision for yourself, to change it to God's ways, laws, and principles. Recognizing that God is in control and we as a people are not, we must submit and commit our lives to him. There really is no other way to live here on this earth. We can live the way we want, and control what we think we should, but we are deceiving ourselves, as this is really not the way things are happening around us.

Acknowledge that God is in Control

Sure, we are to guide people or children, but we are not to control them. God is in control. Your prayers should reflect that God is in control of your life as well as other people's lives. As a parent, it is important to understand that we are to guide our children in what they do and stay away from controlling them. We are to guide them, to keep them safe, and to encourage them. I can see in myself how, at times, I would want to control a situation to just have control, whether it was the right thing to do or not. Control was the ultimate objective. I can ask God to help me and show me ways in which I wanted to control people in the past. Are there ways in which you, dear reader, wanted to have control over other people?

Ask God to bless people whom you are praying for. Acknowledge that God is in control, as he already knows the future. Pray in faith for other people's needs and that God will bless others, praying in faith, with God's joy, by singing, and praising God first and foremost, as though you have already received the answer to the prayer you have prayed.

Sowing and Reaping in Unity

I believe good and bad things happen to people as individuals and in groups because of the reaping and sowing spiritual principle. A group is more powerful, because more people are doing things in unity and agreement. Think for a few moments on how spiritually powerful this is—everyone in unity and agreement for achieving a certain goal for the good of God's kingdom, not the kingdom we are trying to build in whatever we are doing.

"Let's all build God's kingdom together," should be every person's individual and group goal. What an awesome, loving achievement for us to do every chance we get. Ask God how you can build his kingdom. How can you bring people together in unity and agreement to build his kingdom? Focus on these questions, and God will answer your prayer. God's laws, ways, and principles control this world, as he is always in control. It is the hearts of individuals and groups that influence outcomes and events that happen throughout this world. It is beyond our comprehension why things happen the way they do, and it is not up to us to control things for our own purpose. It must be with good intentions, for God's kingdom, or else there is a consequence to pay due to the spiritual principles.

This is why it's so very important to give lovingly and to always do well unto others. One way to think of it is so that we do not receive the same bad treatment, so we can learn to be good people, living with the fruit of Spirit, or we can live the way the world wants to live.

We are really to blame for what happens to us as individuals or as a group. The group can be a family, city, county, state, nation, continent, nationality, religion, country, or any assembly of people. The group has the ability to be blessed or cursed. What a concept!

This is what I have learned by looking at my life and how things have happened to me throughout my life. I just have to accept that God is in control and I am not. Once I realized and understood this, I opened my mind and spirit to God's will and his ways, and not my own.

Build God's Kingdom for His Glory

Remember, we are to build God's kingdom and give him all credit for what we do. Once we start taking credit for anything we do, God will correct or discipline us in a way we can understand. He knows our weaknesses, our strengths, and everything about us. But believe me—the devil knows how to get to you also to serve him. Watch how he plays with you and manipulates you to think that bad thoughts are your thoughts. They are not your thoughts. But since people might think that their minds belong to them and they can only be spoken to from their minds, Satan has a good grip on them, or possibly you, dear reader. One of my goals is to recognize when Satan is playing with me, and to learn how to pray and stop his mind games on me.

Remember, God is good and loving. If the thought be anything else, then I should recognize it is from the dark side of this world, and that is Satan. God is in control, and we have to allow him to control us by his laws, ways, and principles, by changing our speaking and doing unto others, all through our personal choice. By our controlling what we do, and by doing it in all his ways, we set the example for others to follow. This is the light and truth that God wants you to know, dear reader.

Baptism

God wants all his people to be baptized with water, and also to be baptized with the Holy Ghost. Acts 1:5, 8 says, "For John truly baptized with water; but ye shall be baptized with the Holy Ghost not many days hence ... But ye shall receive power, after that the Holy Ghost is come upon you: and ye shall be witnesses unto me both in Jerusalem, and in all Judaea, and in Samaria, and unto the uttermost part of the earth."

God needs leaders and followers who are Christians who have been baptized with water and the Holy Ghost to build his kingdom. What are your strengths, dear reader, and how can you build God's kingdom for him? Are you willing to give your life to serving God? Commit to serving God today, be changed in his ways (not our ways), and enjoy all the fruit of the Spirit that God has to offer. God bless you in all of your endeavors!

Contact Information

For current news and notes of Robin's ministry, please reference the internet website: www.JesusLovesAllofUs.com.

The Holy Spirit touches people in different ways through this publication; therefore, should you feel compelled to provide a financial contribution to distribute books, or to promote and sustain Robin's ministry, please do so. Robin has a heart to contribute funds and to focus on distributing food to the hungry to different parts of the world.